Élisabeth-Pau

The Song]   ^m

On the Mystery of Music

MONASTIC WISDOM SERIES: NUMBER FORTY

The Song That I Am

On the Mystery of Music

An Essay by

Élisabeth-Paule Labat, OSB

Translated by

Erik Varden, OCSO

α

Cistercian Publications
www.cistercianpublications.org

LITURGICAL PRESS
Collegeville, Minnesota
www.litpress.org

A Cistercian Publications title published by Liturgical Press

Cistercian Publications
Editorial Offices
161 Grosvenor Street
Athens, Ohio 45701
www.cistercianpublications.org

This work was orginally published as *Essai sur le mystère de la musique* (Paris: Éditions Fleurus [Mayenne, impr. Floch], 1963). The English translation is done by permission of the abbey of Saint-Michel de Kergonan.

1	2	3	4	5	6	7	8	9

Library of Congress Cataloging-in-Publication Data

Labat, Élisabeth-Paule, author.
    The song that I am : on the mystery of music / an essay by
Elisabeth-Paule Labat ; translated by Erik Varden.
       pages   cm. — (Monastic wisdom series ; no. 40)
    ISBN 978-0-87907-060-1 — ISBN 978-0-87907-680-1 (ebook)
     1. Music—Religious aspects.   2. Music—Philosophy and aesthetics.
I. Varden, Erik, translator.   II. Title.

ML3921.L33 2014
781'.12—dc23   2013047687

Contents

SEDI SAPIENTIÆ
OMNIS HARMONIÆ MAGISTRÆ
VIRGINI MARIÆ
HOC AMANTER DICATUR

Translator's Preface

IN CAPRICCIO, HIS FINAL OPERA, Richard Strauss presented a sophisticated reflection on a problem that has exercised composers since the end of the Renaissance: how can one define the relationship between music and speech, *logos* and *melos*? It was Stefan Zweig who had prompted the composer to address this issue musically, having discovered a precedent in Antonio Salieri's 1786 operetta *Prima la musica, poi le parole*. Being Jewish, Zweig was prohibited from publishing work in post-*Anschluss* Austria. Strauss, however, found a collaborator in Clemens Krauss, who composed the libretto for *Capriccio*, presented as a "conversation piece for music in one act."

In a setting that cleverly mixes allegory and earthy realism, we follow two suitors, the poet Olivier and the composer Flamand, as they woo Madeleine, the lovely Countess, with a joint declaration of love: a poem written by one and set to music by the other. Madeleine is invited to choose him whose statement is truest and most essential. "Music or poetry? Olivier or Flamand?" "*She* will decide," we are told, and the colorful cast assist Madeleine with more or less helpful advice. "The cry of pain preceded speech!" exclaims Flamand, only to hear Olivier retort, "Yet only speech can give pain *meaning*." The Countess remains torn. She sees that her two suitors complement one another; each on his own seems incomplete. "What one of them did not suspect is brought out by the other," says she, sensing a need for both in order to satisfy the requirements of a "heart yearning for beauty."

The drama of *Capriccio* may strike us as agreeable but useless drawing-room chatter, designed to show off overwrought sensibilities. What is more, if we approach the problem it raises from a Christian, biblical viewpoint, the entire to-do is likely to seem superfluous. For, surely, it is beyond doubt that the *Word* "was in the beginning"? So staunch is our adherence to this Johannine dictum that the rebuke of Edwin Muir's poem "The Incarnate One" is often pertinent enough:

> *The Word made flesh here is made word again*
> *A word made word in flourish and arrogant crook.*

The poet's words ring out as a challenge and a provocation. And in the logic of the Incarnation, can we in fact be so sure that theological truth unfailingly follows the principle of *Prima le parole*, that is, that words come first? This is the chief question addressed in this book by a most discerning commentator.

Élisabeth-Paule Labat, a Benedictine nun, was a musician of the highest caliber and a woman of enviable intellectual culture. Throughout her life she sought to grasp what might be the *meaning* of music. She formulated her mature reflection in what remains, perhaps, her most original work, the present *Essay on the Mystery of Music*. When it first came out in 1963, the book was received with delight by, among others, Hans Urs von Balthasar, who recognized in it a "Teresian flight" of the spirit. It is, however, a dense and, to be frank, a difficult work. That is why it has seemed desirable to offer a synoptic analysis of its argument and scope by way of introduction. I shall begin with an outline of Labat's biography, which has a clear bearing on her work. Second, I shall expound the central concern of the *Essay*, namely, the status of music as "language." Is it realistic to maintain that music "speaks" to us? And if so, to what in us does it speak? These questions do not of themselves presuppose faith, and they are treated at first in absolute, neutral terms. Labat goes on, though, to expound them theologically, and this development will take up the third part of my introduction. Finally, in a fourth section, I shall consider the *Essay* as evidencing a peculiarly monastic theology; or better, as orchestrating a monastic testimony. My purpose throughout will be to show how the monastic, contemplative life can facilitate a fruitful dialogue between cultures when the insights of a venerable spiritual tradition are brought to bear on phenomena cultivated in contemporary spheres that it would be too reductive to brush aside as simply "secular." Indeed, certain aspects of a self-proclaimed "sacred" culture may turn out to acquire new splendor from encounters with the unexpected.

♪ ♫ ♪

Paule Labat was born at Tarbes in 1897 into a family of artists and intellectuals. A conventionally religious upbringing left her unequipped to negotiate the pain of life, which soon imposed itself. An encounter with death at the age of five or six left a deep impression, consolidated a little later when a friend of her elder brother's committed suicide. A sense of duty made the little girl pray for him, and this intercession made up the spiritual discipline of her childhood. Meanwhile, she was entering an "irremediable solitude," a growing sense of being "a closed world" from which she yearned to break out. Her intellect demanded to know what underpinned this predicament, and she sought answers in Tolstoy, Dostoyevsky, Claudel—even Renan. Here and there Paule found intimations of a presence, but one that was vague and featureless. The Bible remained a closed book, even when the discovery of Ruusbroec indicated a bridge to link experience and faith. By contrast, the language of music seemed accessible and real.

After the Great War, Paule moved to Paris and enrolled at the Schola Cantorum. There she displayed exceptional promise. Not only was she a brilliant pianist; she wrote music of beauty and originality. A career was opening, yet Paule remained dissatisfied, haunted by the fragility of life. The death of a colleague threw her into such despair that her equilibrium was under threat. It was in this frame of mind that she began the study of Gregorian chant and so discovered an aesthetic and spiritual ambiance that allowed her to breathe. She was impressed by the unsentimental character of this music, by the serenity with which it embraces realities that seem incommensurable. The Offertory *Recordare Virgo Mater* first gave her a sense that fractured lives can find wholeness, that even solitude such as hers need not be final.

Still, with regard to organized religion she remained aloof. If she consented, one day, to look up a local priest, it was simply to humor a pious friend, little suspecting that the encounter would prove decisive. An inner darkness lifted. Paule's cool objections to the Gospel melted before an outpouring of light. The presence that had drawn yet eluded her since childhood had acquired a face at last. She later remarked that there had been "no shadow of exaltation or even surprise, only the impression of total liberation, of a simple, limpid entry into a world that was quite new, yet intimately attuned to me."

In 1922 Paule Labat entered the abbey of Saint-Michel de Kergonan, receiving the name Elisabeth. Many years passed without notable incidents. Sr. Élisabeth became an inspired organist. She was awkward at manual work, absent-minded during ceremonies, generous in community, and uncompromising in fidelity. From the mid-1940s, she produced theological work of substance: at first incidental pieces distributed among friends; later, sustained studies in the form of articles and, eventually, books. Sr. Élisabeth suffered a mild stroke in 1968, five years after writing the *Essay on the Mystery of Music*. A second attack, in June 1972, deprived her of mobility. Conversation became difficult, reading impossible. All at once, she became both dependent and isolated. It was a mode of living to which she did not take easily, certain though she was that it corresponded to the essence of her monastic oblation. Shortly before being struck with paralysis, she made this observation in a notebook:

It is a terrible, terrible thing to feel so utterly estranged from one's surroundings, from creation, from oneself; to be without any consolation human or divine, with a profound sense of impurity and total powerlessness. . . . Everything is falling to pieces. I live without knowing how or why, while my human sensibility has grown ten times more acute. It seems that my vocation to solitude has now reached its fullness— and yet I have never loved others more tenderly. You, Lord, are my boundless desert. I join you in your solitude, which you occupy at the heart of this world that, though you love it with infinite love, remains estranged from you.

She entered the heart of this desert as a place of encounter. Asked whether she was bored, she would answer, "No." Asked whether she missed music, she replied with vigor, "Not at all!" This woman of penetrating intelligence and rare supernatural gifts, of whom it was said, only half in jest, that she "inhabited the stratosphere," was reduced to the most embodied level of existence. On 24 July 1975 she slipped away, into the bright dawn of eternity.[1]

♪ ♫ ♪

From this brief evocation of a life, we may retain two salient features: the recurring experience of solitude and a sense that the mystery of our human condition exceeds comprehension, that it must be received blindly, in darkness, as a gift which only retrospect will reveal as an expression of love. A person refined by such insight will become sensitized to instances of *encounter*, and it is as such that music is first presented in Labat's *Essay*.

In 1943, the requisitioning of Kergonan by German troops obliged the nuns to seek refuge in the nearby manor of Coët-Candec. One evening, as Labat, by then forty-six, was strolling

---

[1] The above information is drawn from an obituary notice of Élisabeth-Paule Labat put together by her monastic community, extant in manuscript only. The archivist of Saint-Michel de Kergonan has kindly put it at my disposal.

in the autumnal splendor of countless shades of gold, music suddenly erupted. This is how she later recalled what took place:

> I had begun to walk beneath the arcades of that enchanted path when I perceived the distant sound of a violin. The more I advanced, the clearer the melody became, and I recognized Mozart's Sonata in E-Minor. From the bow of a proficient performer, the song soared alone with a resonance that seized me to the depth of my soul. . . . Never shall I forget the brief moments I then experienced. I knew that masterpiece by one of music's purest minds of genius. In my youth I had often accompanied it. . . . Yet never had its simple melody seemed charged with such lyricism, such depths of tenderness. Having finished the first movement of the sonata, the violin started again from the beginning. I was still listening.

What had happened? Labat was at pains to say, but even twenty years on she was unafraid to speak of the experience in strong terms. "This exceptional music had torn me quite away from the created world and from myself." It had communicated "contact with the pure essence of music." Indeed, it had been "a revelation of music," imparting both satisfaction and longing. The "revelation" had engaged her intellect as well as her emotions yet "seemed to reveal more of me than feelings woven on the warp of everyday experience and exposed to the clear light of the interior gaze." It had been a presence, a call, a sign—categories that recur throughout the *Essay* as so many signposts.

Labat's engagement with the status of music as language thus arose from a personal experience of being "addressed" by music. For it is of the essence of a "revelation" not to be cast into a void, but to extend from one subject to another. A revelation is "of something" and "to someone." It is fundamentally communicative. If we apply this paradigm to music, there are certainly cases in which we can posit it as transmitting a definite message. We may think of Schumann's *Kinderszenen*, in which each piece evokes a clearly indicated character or mood.

Likewise, we are on reasonably safe ground when dealing with settings of texts, whether in the *Sanctus* of Bach's B-Minor Mass or in a *mélodie* by Fauré. The composer may render the words more or less in accordance with their author's intention (this is the crux of the quarrel between Olivier and Flamand); yet there can be no doubt about his or her intention to communicate *utterance*. Matters become more complex when we enter the realm of pure composition and are left without any attribution of subject. Certainly, we have Cortot's commentaries on the Chopin Preludes (in the Ninth he recognizes the Victory of Samothrace) or Planté's on the *Well-Tempered Clavier*, which charmingly present the B-Flat Minor Fugue as a meeting of drinking companions. Such interpretation can be helpful to performer and listener alike, yet cannot claim the least degree of authority. It is, and must remain, no more than the articulation of suggestive *impressions*.

And music demands more. Labat cites Stravinsky saying, in his *Chronicle of My Life*, that we depreciate music if we love it because we hope to find in it "emotions of joy, pain, or sadness, an evocation of nature, the stuff of dreams." In Stravinsky's vision, music wants to be "a construct of sound, nothing else." Does it then make sense to think of it as a "language"? Does a construct of sound *speak*? Yes, says Labat, but not in ways that accord with commonplace notions of speech. The "language" of music originates in a dimension of consciousness that precedes and transcends articulate reason. We cannot, therefore, expect it to conform to the laws of discourse. Indeed, it is because it draws on *other* registers that it can, without paradox, express the ineffable. Where speech is hampered by its intrinsic linearity, music has means to express opposing themes at the same time and can even unite them in harmonization and counterpoint. Music, then, *is* a language, but a language of signs, not of propositions. Only by approaching it as such shall we find in it a bearer, not just of beauty, but of sense.

These key notions, "sign" and "sense," require some elucidation. Let us begin with "signs." Labat cites Plotinus's vision of the world as εἰκὼν ἀεὶ εἰκονιζόμενος [*sic*], an "ever-imaged image," an *icon* that never ceases to be formed. "Here on earth," she maintains, "everything is a sign." This is not to say, in a vulgar caricature of Plato, that the things we see and hear and touch are somehow not *real*. What Labat is anxious to show is that what we see and hear and touch can never fathom the whole truth of any given thing, which will always, with regard to its origin, for example, or its association with other things, carry messages that elude us. It is the prerogative of poets and contemplatives to intuit this universe of signs and to sense in it (and beyond it) an invisible reality, as in the burning exclamation of Francis Thompson:

> O *world invisible, we view thee,*
> O *world intangible, we touch thee,*
> O *world unknowable, we know thee,*
> *Inapprehensible, we clutch thee!*

Any phenomenon is potentially a sign. But may we perhaps say that music displays this quality to a supreme degree? Its claim to preeminence resides in its imprecision. "Through combinations of sounds that first address our senses, we touch the heart of music only *beyond* realities susceptible of definition." At first hearing, a Debussy Prelude, say, may evoke for us a landscape or a buried emotion. Yet, on analysis, associations evaporate. We are left with nothing but an inexorable "construct of sound," "a few scattered notes cast into the air without leaving more trace than the flight of a bird." Music compels us, after a first appeal to our senses, to seek a more interior reality, the "fulguration of intelligence" from which it springs and which it has power to communicate. Labat is categorical: Anyone who has not been seized by this light— she calls it a "divine" light—"has not yet gained access to music." "Revelation" gives way to "possession." Feeling and understanding are both exceeded. They are portals that may receive music but cannot contain it. That is why genuine music leaves us at once full and dissatisfied. It points beyond itself to a *greater* beauty. And this, precisely this, is the "sense" it communicates, that "the sign of the beautiful is not the beautiful itself, however much it may be bathed in its glory."

♪ ♫ ♪

So far we have reached the following position: our experience of being "addressed" by music makes it legitimate to maintain that music "speaks" to us; insofar as it constitutes a "language" it does not, however, convey logical, linear discourse; its power depends on ambiguity and on a capacity for the simultaneous sounding of opposites; this language of harmonized contrast engages both our intellect and our emotions but cannot be fathomed by either; the fact that music inspires at once satisfaction and hunger shows that it points beyond itself to the source from which it springs; in this respect it is a "sign."

How do we absorb this language? How do we hear it? We *hear* much in the way that we *see*. In a vast perspective, we *look at* one point while *seeing* the rest. Likewise, with music, we may *hear* all the voices but *listen to* one. Labat spells out the implications of this fact by citing a sharp observation made by Georges Duhamel:

> What reaches the deepest, most intimate parts of our being is probably not what lies along the straight line of our attentive understanding, constituting the . . . principal voice. The most delicate phenomena, the ones that defy definition, or better, the *ineffable* phenomena, occur on the margins, in the region of twilight. What we listen to may be sublime, but remains for the most part natural. What we hear, on the other hand, is easily magical and supernatural. The great mystery of music is accomplished outside the scope of direct attention, at the limit of consciousness.

The word "supernatural," aligned to "magical," is here intended literally. It indicates "unconscious" or "beyond the reach

of attention." Labat, however, picks it up and develops it theologically. In a passage that makes us think of Pico della Miran-
dola's vision of man as *contemplator universi* ["beholder of the
universe"], she envisages him as *universi auscultator* ["listener
of the universe"]. "Man is both spiritual and carnal, both rich
and poor, enclosed in himself yet supremely receptive. The
gathered voices of the whole earth rise toward him: he listens
to them, understands them, and makes them his own." This is
the call of music, "to bring together the totality of voices in the
universe and constitute a cosmic act of praise." "Music makes
us cantors on behalf of all creation." We occasionally wake up
to catch a fragment of this doxology. Such moments confirm
our intuition that all things aspire to ultimate unity in a beauty
that is perfect and personal. That is when music fills us at once
with joy and sadness. For as soon as we try to seize hold of
what we hear, we are left bereft.

Our present consciousness is not equipped to contain the
message borne to us. It perceives it at its limit as a tantalizing
possibility, as a call from without that corresponds, remarkably, to waves of yearning surging from within. Appositely,
Labat cites Hildegard of Bingen: *Sed et anima hominis symphoniam in se habet et symphonizans est, unde etiam multotiens planct-
tus educit, cum symphoniam audit, quoniam de patria in exilium
se missam meminit.*[2] Such tears, provoked by music that is truly
a "sign," are not "the effect of our exasperated sensibility."
They are "tears of wonder, born . . . of a recollection that
borders on adoration." In a flash of recognition, they show us
where we come from and where we are going. They indicate
a fugitive homecoming that inspires a more intense longing
for home.

---

[2] "Even the human soul carries symphony and is of its nature sym-
phonic. That is why it is often moved to tears on hearing the symphony
[of music]. It suddenly remembers that it has been sent forth from its
homeland into exile."

In this way the sign-value of music permits it to function as an intermediary. We find it voicing sensibly the "symphony" we carry within. When this occurs, music gives us a sense of belonging. Yet our initial shock of delight turns to grief when we find that the security is not ours to keep. Time and again, Labat speaks of music as a "foretaste" and "promise." A promise of what? Of the *patria*, to speak with Hildegard, or, more specifically, in the words of Augustine, of the "house of God." In his *Enarratio* on the Forty-First Psalm, that great lover of music speaks of the angelic hymn rising everlastingly before the face of God and overspilling into the perplexed muteness of creation, when of a sudden "a mysteriously sweet and musical echo resounds in the soul." "Tickled with delight," says Augustine, the ear thus gifted is drawn irresistibly toward the fullness of sound, like the deer to the spring of water.

The fact that music is a feature of eternity is a *datum* of divine revelation. We have it on biblical authority that angels sing, yet we are unable to imagine *how*. As Labat observes, "Their song is of pure intelligence and could only, it would seem, become sensible through an intervention by the angels themselves, in a gesture of condescension to our carnal condition." Even so, their song would be perceived only by the most interior senses of the soul, duly refined by grace. In his brief, intriguing treatise on *The Song of Angels*, Walter Hilton gives some idea of how such hearing comes about. Labat cites him:

> This song cannot be described by any bodily likeness, for it is spiritual, and above all imagination and reason. It may be felt and perceived in a soul, but it may not be showed. Nevertheless, I will speak of it to you as I think. When a soul is purified by the love of God, illumined by wisdom, and stabilized by the might of God, then the eye of the soul is opened to see spiritual things, as virtues and angels and holy souls, and heavenly things. Then, because it is clean, the soul is able to feel the touching, the speaking of good angels. This touching and speaking is spiritual and not bodily. For when the soul is lifted and ravished out of sensuality, and out of mind

of any earthly things, then in great fervor of love and light
(if our Lord deigns) the soul may hear and feel heavenly
sound, made by the presence of angels in loving God.

To such testimonies, persons vowed to monastic life should
pay close attention. For monks, says Labat, are especially con-
ditioned to hear such singing. It represents the essence of their
calling, which an ancient tradition rightly defines as "angelic."
"Without wanting to become an angel himself, [the monk]
understands that he must become as like one as possible, to
share not only in the angels' song, but in everything that constitutes their life and calling." The self-transcendence to which
he is committed reaches beyond the moral order:

> Its goal is to bring man to praise God, in song and silence,
> by a cry welling up from the innermost core of his being,
> giving voice to his being. Being thus made a "praise of
> glory," he will, in the harmony of his soul, himself become
> pure music. He will gain access to the mystery of music,
> though without ever fathoming it. . . . As man approaches
> the source of music, not as a distant, indefinable *abstractum*
> but as Someone—a someone who is All—he realizes that,
> even here on earth, all is music and all tends towards the
> music of eternity.

It is insofar as we *become* music that we shall penetrate its
mystery, discovering that what it signifies is not a *Quid*
["what"] but a *Quis* ["who"]. This *essential* music is perfectly
compatible with the "concert of silence" spoken of by the
mystics. For the present, however, while still *in via*, we must
content ourselves with scattered fragments of that eternal
symphony as it reaches us through the inspired strains of
earthly music. With Baudelaire, we must be resigned to "our
inability to grasp *now*, wholly here on earth, at once and for
ever, those divine and rapturous joys of which *through* the
poem, *through* the music, we attain to but brief and indeter-
minate glimpses." It is in this sense that Labat, in a tentative

conclusion, speaks of music as a language signifying *"another language,"* which is itself a sign. If we truly love music, we know that we shall one day have to leave it behind, to hear and sing in a new way, as of yet inconceivable. The mystery of music dimly sensed in the present "region of twilight" will sooner or later require *us* as its instruments, using our "soul's movements" to make "a jubilant sound." The language of that *new* song will no longer convey its message "at the limit of consciousness." Once we have made it our own, we shall perceive beauty with the concentrated force of all our faculties, in an encounter face-to-face that is no longer a promise but an eternal possession.

♪ ♫ ♪

The *Essay on the Mystery of Music* was written by a woman with forty years' experience of monastic living. It explicitly states that it is not the work "of a philosopher or theologian, even if its author is not altogether ignorant of philosophy and theology." It is, we are told, a "testimony" inspired by other testimonies. And so it belongs in a genre that, for not being the exclusive property of monks, has always been congenial to them. In this final section, I shall indicate two characteristics of this peculiarly monastic approach to theology.

A first salient feature is the *Essay*'s autobiographical nature. It records an effort stretching over two decades to make sense of a precise moment in the author's life. Yet it does not thereby become a mere chronicle. Apart from the initial account of the encounter with the Mozart Sonata, we are told nothing at all about the circumstances of Labat's life. The experience on which the *Essay* builds is altogether interior and developed with such discretion that we must strain our ears to follow it. When music ceased that evening, nightfall had covered creation with a shroud, leaving the solitary listener bereft, yet radiant with joy. She carried this paradox with her into the dusk, where, we might say, she stayed. The motif of the night

recurs throughout the book, where Sanjuanist allusions sometimes make of it a technical term, as when we hear of the
"succession of nights" by which receptive souls are condi-
tioned for a share in divine light; or of the "purifying night"
that is the mystic's searing pain. At other times the conven-
tional idiom is appropriated, almost subverted, with such
force that a personal urgency is evident. The language of
Scripture merges with that of Rilke and other "poets of the
night" to convey the longing of the Bride who seems to be
abandoned in darkness yet knows that the Bridegroom is
there, invisibly present beyond the lattice wall, his hair moist
with nocturnal dew. Once his presence is perceived, the night
is a "night without darkness"—yet night all the same.

We sense something of the stakes involved in a solitary,
familiar reference to "*my* night," pierced once as by lightning
in a shock of beauty through music. This is appropriate
enough, for music is "a call in the night." Only the night can
teach us to hear it as we ought. Such coded references tell us
more about the drama of the author's life, I think, than any
list of biographical data, though what we know about her life
confirms the code. What might we learn from this? Above all,
the reverence due to any shattering experience of beauty. The
"revelation" of music through Mozart provided Élisabeth-
Paule Labat with a hermeneutical key to her life and vocation.
She applied it perseveringly to the culture that had formed
her mind, excited to find corresponding values in sources that
might appear disconnected: the theological argument of the
Essay owes no less to César Franck and Paul Claudel than to
Augustine and Gregory Nazianzen. The treatment that results
is eclectic and makes few concessions to the reader. But it is
indubitably a "witness," exercising great fascination and possessing, in the Gospel sense, "authority."

The second feature I should like to stress is the eschatological
character of this monastic theology. I do not mean by this that
it reeks of sulphur but that it is resolutely oriented toward the

finality of things. The incident with the E-Minor Sonata is important not for its impact there and then but because it remains a valid pointer toward a greater and final reality. "Today I consider it, that music at once intoxicating and chaste, in the light of the divine realities whose obscure foretaste it was." These realities are by definition beyond our reach, inviting us always to go *further*. We have recognized the autobiographical imprint of the *Essay* in the image of the night. Its eschatological thrust might reasonably be associated with characteristic reference to the sea. From the outset, Labat confesses that she loves the mystery represented by music "too much to forfeit getting out of my depth in the great sea of the unknown into which it plunges me, in order to remain there always, without ever finding my way back to the shore." Music is apt to evoke this mystery because it rests in an immensity of silence that "envelops and suffuses it like a great sea." The beauty we find in it refreshes us and sets us free "like a great gust of sea-breeze instantly sweeping away our earthbound attachments." Yet the full force of these realities will appear only in the life to come, when we shall respond to it in the angelic language of which music is, here below, a sign. It is a language of silence, but a "*positive* silence, a silence which indicates not absence but presence." At that point we shall no longer need signs, being "bathed in the sea of reality, . . . in the presence of him who *is*." The tensions that constitute earthly music will be resolved in a new song in which

> serene transparency and the balance of repose will be at one with the vital, vehement energy rushing forth from the depths of divinized being. . . . The symphony of the saints will be marked by neither tragedy nor pathos. Yet all that is truly great in tragedy and pathos will resonate within it, bathed in perfect peace, like an immense surge that rises from the bottom of the sea yet spreads upon the surface in gentle ripples. This, I think, is what the music of eternity will be like.

The promise heralded by Mozart will be redeemed in that concert, under the direction of Christ, "the great harmonizer of the visible and invisible cosmos." We shall no longer experience music. Music will be what we are.

♪ ♫ ♪

As a final point, it may be useful to recall that *The Essay on the Mystery of Music* was written in 1963, while the Second Vatican Council was in session. The "inculturation" of monasticism was a priority on many a monk's and nun's agenda. Labat's book stands for a complementary, not contradictory, trend. We might call it a "monastification" of culture. With intelligence and reverence, she approaches the mystery of music in the light of the monastic mystery, assimilating it within the parameters of a rich spiritual tradition. This procedure contributes to the book's status as a "testimony." Yet it is also an "essay," and we are entitled to interpret this term quite as Montaigne intended it. What Labat holds out to us is a sketch, a work-in-progress, an offering that invites response. This dialogic, nondogmatic trait is an attractive aspect of monastic theology, which enjoys a more flexible range than that imposed by the austere requirements of the schools. Precisely because it *is* free and off-beat, it can come up with insights that are fresh and illuminating.

In the grandiose monologue that brings *Capriccio* to a close, the Countess expresses her inability to perform the task set before her. Word and music, Olivier and Flamand, appear so intrinsically connected that the composer's plea—*Prima la musica!*—fills her with consternation. "Can there," she asks, "be a conclusion [to this problem] that is not trivial?" Élisabeth-Paule Labat shows us that, yes, there can. She presents *one* answer, not *the* answer, but it is one that deserves (and repays) consideration. The category of "sign" allows her to go beyond juxtaposition, to *articulate* the mystery of music in a way that is both coherent and profound. And it could be that the quandary of Madeleine ultimately rests on insufficiently defined terms. As Cardinal Newman reflected as an old man, in a letter cited in the *Essay*: "Perhaps thought *is* music?" And if so, would it be so far-fetched to think that the *Logos* of "the beginning" is present and manifest also as *Melos*? After the death of Élisabeth-Paule Labat, Louis Bouyer wrote of her as follows in his preface to her posthumous volume *Présences de Dieu*:

> The harmony of this monastic soul, so profoundly delicate and sensitive, overcame the dissonances of this present life by assuming them, presaging the peace of eternity—the faithful echo of a Presence sensed and acknowledged that claimed her entirely for itself.[3]

It is striking that Bouyer, a man of such profound intuition, should evoke Labat by means of a musical metaphor. The "essential music" to which she aspired had taken possession of her even before she plunged fully into the "sea of God." It had resounded in the "night" where, if we will, we can hear it still.

Erik Varden, OCSO
Feast of the Transfiguration, 2012[4]

---

[3] *Présences de Dieu*, par une moniale bénédictine, préface de Louis Bouyer (Paris: Fayard, 1979), 2.

[4] This preface is an adaptation of a paper printed in *Monasticism between Culture and Cultures*, ed. Philippe Nouzille and Michaela Pfeifer, *Studia Anselmiana* 159 (Rome: Pontificio Ateneo S. Anselmo, 2013). The material is reproduced here by kind permission of the editors. —Ed.

Introduction

IT SEEMS OPPORTUNE to introduce this *Essay* by revealing not only the goal it pursues but the circumstances that caused it to be written. Its point of departure was an apparently fortuitous adventure that occurred during the war of 1940–45 when, fleeing the German occupation, I found refuge in a vast old château near Vannes, in that wonderfully undulating forested region defined from afar by the bell tower of Grandchamp.

One fine October evening, I was, as so often, making my way through a rickety side gate toward the rampart, accessible by a small stairway. To take in the narrow circular avenue that wound its way through a double row of beeches and chestnuts passing from every shade of brilliant to pale gold was, as every day, a wonder. I had begun to walk beneath the arcades of that enchanted path when I perceived the distant sound of a violin. The more I advanced, the clearer the melody became, and I soon recognized Mozart's Sonata in E-Minor. From the bow of a proficient performer, the song soared alone with a resonance that seized me to the depth of my soul. I understood that it issued from a massive watchtower rising before me, its enormous base rooted in the moat. Never shall I forget the brief moments I then experienced. I knew that masterpiece by one of music's purest minds of genius. In my youth I had often accompanied the dear sonata, which one never tires of playing and which, for me, will always carry memories of home. Yet never had its simple melody seemed charged with such lyricism, such depths of tenderness. Having finished the first movement of the sonata, the violin started again from the beginning. I was still listening.

It was already late, and at that hour when, as if with a presentiment of approaching nightfall, nature appears to recollect itself and become immaterial, this exceptional music had torn me quite away from the created world and from myself. When the voice of the violin fell silent and the spell was broken, it seemed that those few minutes—more than hours (in themselves unforgettable) spent listening to performances by the very greatest musicians—had been to me, through contact with the pure essence of Beauty, a revelation of music.

What was the mystery which this enchanting music conveyed? What secret message disclosed itself through a few scattered notes cast into the air without leaving more trace than the flight of a bird? Was it the loving heart of Mozart that, through the chasm separating life from death, spoke to my heart, thus surviving itself here below? Or was it the echo of a paradise lost of happiness and innocence that reached me, the unspeakable language of something divine akin to my innermost being, permeating me with an obscure feeling at once of satisfaction and longing? How to account for a joy that, for being pure, was heartrending, for an emotion felt beyond the clear consciousness of self, which nonetheless seemed to reveal more of me than feelings woven on the warp of everyday experience and exposed to the clear light of the interior gaze?

These questions were pressing on my mind as I walked back, wrapped in the peace of that lovely autumn evening. And I remembered a phrase read long ago: "Music is not the sum of written scores. It is something eternal to which they allude." I conceived then the desire to make some humble effort to understand the mystery of music, a mystery all the more arresting for touching other facets of the unknown on which it may, perhaps, shed light: the unknown of our soul, which is its subject; and the unknown of the invisible world where our deepest being is rooted, concealed from us here below by the veil of created things. Any design to scrutinize this mystery to the point of dispelling mystery would, of course, be absurd, a rash and foolish enterprise. Would we not, to the extent that we entered its secrets, be bound to see it elude our grasp and retreat to an inaccessible Beyond? Yet I love the mystery too much to forfeit getting out of my depth in the great sea of the unknown into which it plunges me, in order to remain there always, without ever finding my way back to the shore. And may we not hope that a clearer, deeper awareness of the implications of the mystery of music will attune our soul to realities that, though exceeding our capacity, touch what is highest and most sacred in the life of the mind?

The present essay does not claim to be the work of a great thinker, of a philosopher or theologian, even if its author is not altogether ignorant of philosophy and theology. It is merely a personal testimony. As such, it would be worthless were it not based on other testimonies of greater authority, from that of Saint Augustine to those of Marcel de Corte, Erik Peterson, and Jacques Maritain; were it not, further, calling on eternal truths that are simple, profound, and too often neglected. It is also a testimony of love. I am conscious of all that I owe to this sovereign music, which, like the air I breathe, has surrounded and penetrated my entire life with its mysterious influence. From childhood music has, more than the wonderful world found in books, been for me supremely the land of poetry and dreams—dreams at one with a reality that, though hidden, is the greatest there is.

During long hours spent at the piano rehearsing, music held me captive. It mattered little whether it was sad or joyful, spirited or calm. I suspected that the gamut of feelings vibrating within it, springing from a range of souls, from many kinds of genius, expressed only superficial modalities, swirls of an ocean of life and love whose depths I wished to plumb in order to immerse myself in them. The universe of Bach was closed to me still. My favorite composer was Beethoven. I tirelessly reread his Life, as well as Romain Rolland's study of him. My ambition was one day to play all the sonatas. I dreamt naïvely of being the woman who, by understanding this tormented genius, might by a love stronger than fate have brought a light of joy and supernatural grace into the life of a titan distressed.

After Beethoven, I came to love Schumann best. It was at the time when Ravel and Debussy formed the avant-garde and when the dissonances of Claude de France struck me as deliciously bold. Dear music! How it consoled me in suffering! What a friend it was in solitude! With its capacity for interiorization, unmatched in the created order, it was, I think, thanks to it, to its slow, sweet penetration, that a distaste was born in me for all that is superficial, vulgar, and false, accompanied by the desire for a spiritual paradise of an ideal presence, before which every earthly presence would wear away. Yes, music was truly, before the dawn of grace, the distant but persuasive voice of a supernatural something that points the way without revealing, portends without yielding its secret, leaves one saturated with happiness yet unfulfilled. Today I consider it, that music at once intoxicating and chaste, in the light of divine realities whose obscure foretaste it was. Even as the world of grace lets us understand the world of nature, of which it is the crown, allowing us to discover nature's splendors, it is with the limitless, transparent perspectives of the kingdom of God, of God living among us and within us, that I glimpse the meaning of art and the grandeur of its message.

To this observation, however, something else must be added. When it does not betray its mission, music leads us, by a grace preceding grace, beyond ourselves to the land of oneness and life only at the price of separation and death. Music is indeed remembrance of an earthly paradise, for which it can inspire only useless nostalgia. But its real purpose is to draw us toward a heavenly paradise that can be entered solely at the cost of boundless detachment. That is why its call at once represents soothing and disquiet, joy and pain. When received by an attentive, receptive soul, its message inaugurates a new life of renunciation. The true design of this sovereign music is to tear us away from the world while leading us—at the heart of the world, by it and through it—toward him by whom the world subsists, who lives infinitely beyond the world yet is constantly present to it: toward God. Let us not forget that we inhabit a universe of sin, that God, infinite Holiness, Beauty, Goodness, and Light can only be reached by those who pass through the great waters of death like Christ, our Pasch. We are part of his body as much in its humiliation as in its glory, as much in its suffering as in its joy.

My testimony is also a testimony of love. I have written and published it on the advice of friends because I thought it might be of use to certain souls. It is indeed the testimony of one heart speaking to another: *Cor ad cor loquitur.* Certainly, it makes no claim to perfection. May its very shortcomings and the criticism it will raise incite minds clearer by their vigor and learning to complete it, to sharpen its focus for the good of souls and the glory of God, who is Love, the Love that created music and finds in music possibly its purest means of self-expression.

A certain number of repetitions mark this work. For these I apologize. I have let them remain in the conviction that some, if not all, may serve a purpose. Certain truths need, by virtue of their importance, to be called to mind again and again; others, which to begin with are only indicated, are set in deeper relief and acquire greater significance as our perspective either broadens or narrows. They are intrinsic to the development of a line of thought that is ceaselessly seeking itself. The present essay is the record of such seeking. That is how it is offered, in testimony, to the public.

On Music Considered as Language

MUSIC CONSTITUTES A UNIQUE, IRREPLACEABLE LANGUAGE. In Malègue's novel *Augustin*, one character remarks after hearing a masterpiece: "How one would love great musicians to speak of the feelings they carry in their heart!" His interlocutor responds: "If they could, there would be no need for music." There are in man, in the secret of his soul as well as in his relations with both the invisible and the visible world, depths and nuances that words are powerless to express. It is the mission of music to convey them. Like the spoken word, music draws from the wellspring of silence. But the silence whence it springs and toward which it leads us never leaves it; it envelops and suffuses it like a great sea. Thus music is the homeland of mystery; the echo of an unknown world beyond clear ideas and defined feelings.

It is likewise a unique, irreplaceable language by virtue of the effectiveness and suddenness with which it seizes, charms, and arrests us. It seems to bring about a real dispossession of self by stealing into the innermost recesses of our soul. It wants us to collude with it, yet does not lord it over us in the manner of a despot. If this sovereign music invades us, gently and forcefully, it is to take us not only beyond ourselves but beyond *it*self.

I propose that we begin our enquiry by considering music as a language communicating an ineffable spiritual content. From there we shall proceed to the threshold of what Saint Augustine, at the end of his treatise *De musica*, calls the *secretissima* ["most hidden recesses"], the *penetralia* ["innermost

1

shrine"], the *cubilia* ["marriage bed"] of music, to the most hidden sanctuary where dwells the sovereign Unity, the *unum principale,* from which every number, and therefore all music, pours forth. For as the great Doctor declares, numbers indisputably reign over music. Sound is, so to speak, the light of these numbers that, without it, would remain silent.[1]

---

[1] *In hoc igitur quarto gradu sive in rhythmis sive in ipsa modulatione intellegebat regnare numeros totumque perficere* (*De ordine* II.14). Cf. *De musica* VI.13: . . . *in ipso sono qui quasi lux est talium numerorum cui sic est contrarium silentium ut colores tenebrae.* It should be pointed out that the word *musica* meant something other to Saint Augustine than it does to us. He considered *musica,* which he defines, probably following Varro, as *scientia bene modulandi,* as a technique based on notions of number rather than as an art in the modern sense of that word, that is, as a sensible expression of the beautiful. Augustine's conception of *musica* was primarily rational, and when he speaks about it in order to integrate it into his vision of culture, it is as a philosopher of the Neo-Platonic cast (cf. H.-I. Marrou, *Saint Augustin et la fin de la culture antique* [Paris: Boccard, 1938], 197–204). This is why an uninformed reader launching into the treatise *De musica,* even the sixth book, which is the most accessible and most profound, suspects a kind of misunderstanding between himself and the author. Everything becomes clear once he grasps the difference between Augustine's notion of music and that of a modern musician, for whom music is a matter of aesthetics, not of reason or morals. We should further bear in mind the author's pedagogical aim, which is clearly stated in the first chapter of the same book. Then, if we attentively follow Augustine as he differentiates between different kinds of "numbers," passing from sensible numbers to spiritual and eternal numbers; if we see a general notion of "number" implying relation, harmony, order, and tendency to unity expand and free itself from anything created to the point of reaching the mystery of the Blessed Trinity, the perfect Unity from which, in the world of spirits as in our own world of bodies, every harmony, every relation, every order, every tendency to unity springs (*De musica* VI.17), we glimpse horizons that are surely far from alien to our aesthetic notion of music, provided we pass beyond the signs to the reality they signify, discovering the deepest meaning of music's language and mission. Finally, we may remark that Augustine's fine sensibility did not escape the attraction of music, as many passages in his works (including *Confessions* X.33) testify. The word *cantare* often recurs, notably in the *Enarrationes in Psalmos.* For Augustine, it aptly

Without pretending to trace here the origin and development of music, we can point to its first manifestations and ask how, as a primordial element of sound, it came to claim man's attention. Would we not say that it was first discerned in the varied inflexions of human language no less than in the innumerable sounds of the natural world? Words are made to express ideas. That is why man alone among the beings that inhabit the earth has the privilege of possessing them. Created in the image of the likeness of God, he takes after his Creator (who has but one Word, substantial and perfect, by which he speaks himself entirely) in communicating verbally. On account of his imperfection, however, for he is always in a state of becoming, it is not with a single word that he translates the world of his thoughts and feelings, but by a succession of multiple and ephemeral words. If words are made to express ideas, the human voice that utters them has the power, in itself magnificent, to invest them with fervor and conviction. By its many nuances it reveals the movements of our heart and sensibility, the promptings of our will in dialogue with clear reason. Is there not a potential music in the dynamic and tonal variations impressed on simple speech by the emotion that carries it, whether discreetly or with vehemence?

Cicero observed that there is in speech a *cantus obscurior,* which is to say that words contain the seed of a melody that is capable, through art, of expansion and freedom. Man is instinctively drawn by beauty. He is pressed by the need to exteriorize as adequately as possible that which lives in him. He is attentive to the noblest ways in which beauty beckons him. It is not strange, therefore, that he should soon draw a distinction between sound itself and the ideas expressed by sound.[2]

---

renders a soul's irresistible need to pour forth in praise all the feelings to which deeply experienced religious emotion may give rise: enthusiasm, desire, regret, discreet or overflowing joy, etc.

[2] The remark comes from Augustine's treatise *De ordine,* dating from before his baptism, where he attempts to account for the genesis of

At the same time, man perceived sound throughout the humblest and most familiar voices of nature, in the solemn, persistent chant of the sea and in the twittering of birds rejoicing to be alive, the nightingale's airs, or the song of "crickets beginning, with little chirps, to burn" (Jules Laforgue). Although these voices are evocative for any soul with a sense of poetry, they are not properly speaking music, for music arises in the exteriorization through sound of the secret vibrations of a soul. Yet it is through the datum of sound that man, equipped not only to listen but to discern—to distinguish intervals, rhythms, harmonies, and pitch—lays hold of these elements, combines them, and is able to make from them a language suffused with his own mind and heart.

Let us consider the effect of sound on our capacity for attention. Any sound, especially one endowed with beauty, will keep us listening, as if to call forth in us an interior silence to echo itself, beyond what is sensible. Think of a bell sounding in the peace and harmony of the evening. Does it not invite recollection? It has been correctly pointed out, too, that the phenomenon of sound as simple interjection constitutes the most immediate expressions of the soul, the voicing, we might say, of its Ohs! and Ahs! It presents us with an objectification of the soul by and for itself, an expression that occupies the middle ground between unconscious concentration and the return to self by means of deliberate interior thought.

If this can pertain to isolated sounds, how much more will a succession of sounds, following the creative movement of the mind and the laws of melody and rhythm, be endowed with the twofold potential to express and interiorize the soul, still in the undefined domain of a zone that sits deeper than that in which clear ideas are elaborated? The spoken word itself, when it is warm, harmonious, and supple, possesses

---

music: *At ista [ratio] potentissima secernendi cito vidit, quid inter sonum et id, cuius signum esset, distaret* (II.14).

penetrating power. Think, then, what can be wrought when melody raises the word into flight by espousing it, conforming the word to its own color, to its movement, ardor, and peace? Melody surrounds the word with an atmosphere of soul that is intimate and communicative, from which one heart of flesh gains the power to touch another, to make it vibrate in union with itself. "Song," said Thomas Carlyle, is "the Heroic of speech."[3] It is the aspect of speech that not only touches and convinces but ennobles, exalts, and empowers.

By way of example we may (without yet considering the admirable Gregorian cantilena, which possesses a special charism as much through its sacred character as through its mission) recall certain popular songs that are wonderfully expressive in their simplicity: that of the Volga boatmen, for example, with its nostalgic, almost savage beauty, or any number of Celtic or Breton chants imbued with exquisite tenderness and otherworldly melancholy.

At this point, we cannot fail to mention the reciprocal role of the two elements of music: melody and rhythm. It would be futile to enter upon technical considerations. But we can go a step further. Concerning rhythm we should note, first of all, that man finds it and submits to it everywhere, both within himself and around him. Only the force of habit can blunt our awareness of the universal force of rhythm regulating our physical being and the exercise of our faculties, even as it regulates every other circulating and evolving thing, everything that endures, from the alternation of hours, days, and seasons to the bowing down of a branch bent by the weight of its fruit or by a gust of wind. Rhythm is imprinted on our body in our heartbeats, in the alternating inhalation and exhalation of our breathing, and in our movement when we walk or otherwise

---

[3] *On Heroes, Hero-Worship, and the Heroic in History* [a reprint of the "Sterling Edition" of Carlyle's Complete Works, in twenty volumes] (Middlesex: Echo, 2007), 58.

use our members. What we have here is rhythm in time. But there is also a spatial rhythm that informs the structure of our bodies.[4] Everything on earth is subject to the power of rhythm, even animals. The Bedouin journeying through the desert marks the camels' slow pacing with his singsong.

Finally, in a hidden but nonetheless real way, rhythm presides over the vital manifestations of the human soul. Saint Augustine has magisterially shown how there is a spiritual rhythm submitted to the laws of numbers, even if these numbers escape the control of our senses. This is important. The soul possesses a hidden rhythm of its own at its most secret depths, where it is unknown to itself and seen only by God and his angels. There it lives in communion with the invisible world, not through any sensible contact but in the highest point of its being, in total dependence on its Creator. There are other rhythms whose progress and cadences the soul can more or less perceive in that region where its thoughts and acts of will are worked out, where it is subject to reactions of desire or aversion prompted by its relations to people and things, where it expresses itself successively as tension and possession, energy and rest. If the soul did not have within itself an intelligible rhythm derived from the rhythm of uncreated Wisdom "reaching forcefully from end to end and gently arranging all things" (Wis 8:1), it could not appreciate or judge the rhythms it perceives outside itself. Saint Augustine teaches us that these mysterious numbers of "discernment" have greater dignity than sensible numbers. Thus the soul's intelligible rhythm exercises its sovereignty over poetic or musical rhythms. This is not the place to insist further on that immanent rhythm, which, by informing a melody that is likewise intelligible, creates an ontological, existential music whose mysterious, silent resonances any true music is called to awaken.

---

[4] More precisely, corporeal movements develop rhythmically in both time *and* space. Dance provides a striking illustration.

Rhythm, then, constitutes the masculine, active element in music: an "ordering of movement" in Plato's definition; "proportion in time" according to Vincent d'Indy. It exercises its influence on a melody that represents the feminine, passive element. When melody appears with its all-embracing mobility and graceful inflexions, with the pondered or spontaneous variety of movements gently led or broken, with the charm of its timbre, rhythm is there to embrace it. Whether its touch is domineering or delicate, it is always sure and precise, manfully ordering and coordinating sounds. It infuses them with life through working their synthesis. The melody's curves may be capricious or austere; rhythm follows, maintaining balance and discipline while bestowing definite form and beauty. Without rhythm, melody would be but a dust of sounds. The melody in its turn flows out upon rhythm and frees it from possessiveness, raising it above the earth. At one moment, it may give rhythm wings, granting it access to regions of fantasy, of the ideal; at another it brings it to depths more akin to silence; it incites energy, then calm; and sometimes it hardly stirs at all, asking rhythm to keep it in a sphere of rest, discretion, and recollection where it is pleased to dwell.

Thus the opposition and interpenetration of the masculine and feminine elements—one of the great laws of life that ensures its flourishing, completion, fecundity, and joy—is imprinted on the heart of music. It presides over that which is most essential, most at one. Surely we can locate the foundation of all music in this encounter of an element of proportion and balance with an element of spontaneity and grace: a first manifestation of the alliance between order and love that characterizes all true art, any truly great work of poetry or music.[5]

---

[5] The law of union between the masculine and feminine elements in music can be recognized in certain forms of composition, notably in the first sonata movement, where two themes of different character engage. Once presented, they enter into a kind of battle whose character is sometimes grandiose and charged with pathos, leading to the victory of the

Combining their resources at the service of man's creative faculties, rhythm and melody prepare the emancipation of music. For why should it remain bound to words? Of course, it will always be able to bestow on words an unsuspected impetus, to become one with them in the composition of great works of art. But music is awakening to its autonomy. It knows that it constitutes, by itself, a language that transcends all others.

Even when reduced to a single voice, music possesses remarkable means of expression. We may think of any number of solo pieces for the violin or flute, or of Henri de Régnier's humble reed pipe, able to express the soul of all nature's harmonies:

> *A single reed sufficed for me*
> *To make the tall grass sing,*
> *Likewise the field*
> *And the gentle willows.*
> *A single reed sufficed for me*
> *To make the forest sing.*

In a higher sphere, let us think of some ornate Gregorian piece where the cantilena suddenly seems to leave behind the text that first inspired it in order to become pure vocalization. Such remarkable purity in adoration, supplication, and praise is charged with a spiritual density that can hardly be surpassed. We find it in many an Alleluia jubilus overflowing

---

masculine motive, enriched by the meeting with its counterpart. By way of example, who has not been struck by the gripping opposition between the opening beats, as implacable as fate, of the initial theme of Beethoven's Fifth Symphony and the profound acquiescence, gentleness, and surrender of the succeeding feminine theme? The drama played out in that immortal monument is based on the contrast. It is a drama profoundly human, yet touched by eternal resonance. One thinks likewise of the vicissitudes, successively insinuating or passionate, discreet or majestic, that define César Franck's Third Organ Chorale, which ends with the triumphant affirmation of the initial theme.

with grave or exultant happiness, in Offertories such as the admirable *Recordare*, the *Stetit Angelus* of the Mass of Saint Michael the Archangel, or the great *Iubilate* of the Second Sunday after Epiphany, indeed in all pieces where at a given moment, delivered to its own inspiration, music takes wing and soars.

Music is not content, however, with this emancipation from the word, and here a new stage opens with vast implications. To express its message to the full, music needs not only a single voice but a combination of voices that, either moving together like a marching column of troops (harmony) or simultaneously pursuing their progress with a mixture of solidarity and independence (counterpoint), effect the full unravelling of its riches, whether in a simple duet or in a full symphony of combined choir and orchestra. The development takes place because the soul is simultaneously one and complex. While it remains ever the same in its deepest identity, what a multitude of voices vibrate and sing within it! Man is both spiritual and carnal, both rich and poor, enclosed in himself yet supremely receptive. The gathered voices of the whole earth rise toward him: he listens to them, understands them, and makes them his own. His innermost core also resounds with the voices of heaven and the invisible world. These he attunes to the voices that sing within him and about him. All that sounds in the depth of his mind, in the less hidden sphere of his sensibility, all that echoes within him, must be set in motion through the horizontal and vertical simultaneity of voices. Often, a symphony's most moving beauty is found in the region of mystery where the gentlest voices let themselves be heard, accompanying the sovereign melody. Georges Duhamel accounts for this phenomenon in a few striking lines. Even as in a vast perspective, he says, we look at only one point while seeing the rest, so, when exposed to polyphony, "we hear all the voices but listen to one."

There follows a remark that merits attention:

What reaches the deepest, most intimate parts of our being is probably not what lies along the straight line of our attentive understanding, constituting the essential message or, in music (as students would say), the principal voice. The most delicate phenomena, the ones that defy definition, or better, the *ineffable* phenomena, occur on the margins, in the region of twilight. What we listen to might be sublime, but remains for the most part natural. What we hear, on the other hand, is easily magical and supernatural. The great mystery of music is accomplished outside the scope of direct attention, at the limits of consciousness.[6]

We now have before us the language of music equipped with all its elements. The music of this earth has become, as it were, the prelude, the foretaste of the mighty voice of great waters that flows into the canticles of the Apocalypse because the very highest and the very deepest voices are enabled to melt into a splendor of unity; because this music will give rise to cathedrals of sound like the major works of Bach or Beethoven's Ninth; because vast orchestras will at once combine and contrast the timbre of their instruments as if to bring together all the voices of the universe in a cosmic act of praise.

Because music is essentially a living art, it will always move toward new forms and new means of expression based on the foundations of melody, rhythm, and harmony. In the measure that mankind matures and becomes more conscious of itself, of the poignant, complex character of its destiny, it seeks in music—of all the arts most fit to convey its defining aspirations—ever new resources to express human life, love, and desire. Thus, from the primitive yet perfect art of the Gregorian cantilena and the early motets to the art of Honegger and Stravinsky, music will always be looking for something more supple and subtle in its rhythm, for new colors of modality, for more suggestive voicing, for harmonies that are richer, bolder, more immaterial.

[6] *La Musique consolatrice* (Monaco: Le Rocher, 1989), 153, 155.

It is time to make a preliminary but essential observation. The artist's genius creates brilliance of form through rhythmic, melodic, and harmonic combinations of sounds. These combinations are of their nature indefinite. We thus find that the sounds are essentially signs of another language in whose regard we shall see, later, that it is itself a sign.

♩ ♫ ♩

Let us stay with the question of "signs." It will open perspectives that we shall only have to follow step by step in order to gain access to the mystery that is signified. What do I mean by speaking of sounds as signs? Only this: that sounds, like the lines and colors of a picture or the words of a poem, should not merely be considered in themselves, as so many *things,* but also as means destined to reveal something else, something that, as signs, they spontaneously represent.

When sonorous signs first address and captivate our senses, it is not in order to keep us on their level but to obtain the senses' permission to free our mind, to make it apt to receive the message of a mysterious beauty that tends to carry the soul beyond the created order. The composer's special calling is to create and combine signs so that, with the help of sonorous symbols, he may lead fellow human beings to communion with the music that springs forth, by inspiration, from the silent wellspring of his being.

The signs are endowed with a twofold power of expression and impression. They are expressive insofar as they translate what stirs and sings in the depth of the artist's heart; they are impressive because they possess a penetrating, possessive power by means of which the musical idea steals into a receptive soul, not only to touch and delight it, but also to give rise to an interior music like that dictated by inspiration to the artist's heart *before* he translated it through signs.

Thus, thanks to sonorous signs, a mysterious communication is established invisibly between the artist's soul and other souls: the artist, moved by creative inspiration, puts all the resources of his genius and learning at inspiration's disposal, not to be constrained by it, but in order not to betray it; his audience will be more or less receptive according to their natural capacity for beauty, their aptitude for appreciating art, their level of interiority. While the signs pass through our senses toward the soul, the soul itself opens. This does not occur by any process or effort of abstraction, but passively, intuitively, as the soul receives the persuasive power of the signs and delivers them of their spiritual content so as to make this content its own.[7]

♩ ♫ ♩

What makes up the spiritual content of musical signs? This question has often given rise to controversy. The problem does not, at first sight, seem to admit a simple solution. Some think that music exists to express feelings, even as speech is destined to convey thoughts. "While reason speaks, love sings," said Joseph de Maistre. Others point out, not unreasonably, that music, on account of its imprecise character, is unfit to render this or that feeling considered in its substance, and that its mission is rather to express the dynamic, kinetic aspect of feeling.[8] And surely it is true that our various passions are marked by different modalities? Love, for example, may be calm or impetuous, joyful or sad without ceasing to be love. Being an art of movement, music is apt to render those movements of soul that are not the substance of a feeling but rather expressions of the infinity of nuances a feeling may assume.

---

[7] On the question of the beautiful, of the impact of form that, while in itself intelligible, is seized through and by the senses, see Jacques Maritain, *Art and Scholasticism*, trans. J. F. Scanlan (London: Sheed & Ward, 1946), 21, 124ff.

[8] See P. Ferreti, *Esthétique grégorienne* (Paris, Tournai, Rome: Desclée et Cie, 1938), 125–26.

For this reason it happens that an emotion arising out of a piece of music may be attributed to more than a single passion, for it is not exclusively bound to any one. Who could tell me, say, the defining feeling behind a Bach chorale breathing sheer joy and serenity if I were unacquainted with the text that had inspired it? Does it reflect a tender soul's rest in the beloved? Or rather the solemn, supremely calm joy that follows a great act of detachment, savored in solitude of heart? How can I know whether the triumphant impetuosity that marks the finale of a Beethoven symphony expresses a superhuman energy, owning itself and raising itself up to the realm of the sublime in order to subdue a tragic destiny; or whether it evokes, rather, the invincible enthusiasm of faith founded on the very ruins of despair, beyond the bounds of human possibilities?[9]

But let us look at another, quite different interpretation of the language of music. In his *Chronicle of My Life*, Stravinsky, a musician of genius, declares that we depreciate music if we love it, as most people do, because we hope to find in it emotions of joy, pain, or sadness, an evocation of nature, the stuff of dreams, or a means to escape our prosaic existence. Music would not be worth a great deal if reduced to such a purpose. In Stravinsky's vision, expounded by A. Gasco, "music is incapable of expressing any feeling whatever, and it is madness to harbor illusions in this regard. Music wants to be a construct of sound, nothing else."

---

[9] This imprecise character of music explains why great composers— Bach or Mozart—did not hesitate to apply a melody written for a given text to other words and how the melody lost nothing in the transfer. It likewise legitimates the frequent adaptations we find in Gregorian chant. If some invite criticism (such as the adaptation of the Communion of Pentecost to that of Corpus Christi), others are so felicitous that it is impossible to discern the type from subsequent versions. A good example is the adaptation of the Offertory chant *Stetit* for Saint Michael to the words of *Iustorum animae*, the Offertory for the Common of Martyrs. One likewise thinks of the Graduals of the type *Iustus*.

We may find this perspective disconcerting and rather brutal. Yet Stravinsky is surely not wrong to react against a conception of music that lowers it beneath itself through failing to recognize the authentic message of music, whose source lies beyond human feelings, even the noblest, in an unfathomable absolute. But is it necessary, in order to safeguard the profound and mysterious meaning of music, to deny it any potential to express the soul's emotions? Are we obliged to opt for one theory at the expense of the other? I think not. Between these points of view there is no contradiction but a movement below the surface of music toward its heart, toward the *secretissima* to which we have already alluded. While music does render feeling, or rather, the kinetic aspect of feeling, it *is* at a deeper level a pure construct of sound that transcends any stirring, any disposition of the heart. In its unity, it constitutes a language that is remarkably rich and complex, simultaneously distant and immediate. As we shall see later, music springs from the depth of the soul, where the soul itself, alongside all other beings, is in communion with Being, Beauty, Life. But in order to reach us and take us back to its hidden source, it must pass through the mind and heart of man. Therefore it brings us not only a message from a mysterious beyond but also the most intimate inclinations, the most delicate vibrations of man's own sensibility and interior life.

For this reason, any work of genius will maintain an anonymous or universal character while nonetheless bearing the imprint of its author. The waters of different currents mingle in it: of a race, a history, a landscape, a line of descent, a temperament, a destiny. All are in evidence, and knowledge of these elements may help our understanding of the whole. But beyond them dawns the eternal human soul, transfigured by the divine light that passes through it and surrenders its secret through the color of earthly contingencies. Is it not precisely insofar as a work of art is at once personal *and* pregnant with life transcending its author that it will endure, that it will be great and endowed with what we think of as "character"?

And is it not because the movements of soul expressed by music rest on a reality that transcends, surrounds, and quickens them that they cannot be rendered in any other language except that of sound? Beyond the gamut of emotions and feelings there is something essential: an access opening onto the invisible and eternal; contact established with a world that corresponds to our innermost aspirations. Is this not why music captivates us and invades us with an indefinable impression of fullness, with a solemn, essentially unique joy?

♩ ♫ ♩

To help us better understand the spiritual content of musical signs, it will perhaps not be vain to draw a comparison from a sphere that is higher for being, in the strict sense of the term, supernatural. In Dante's phrase, "art is the grandchild of God." We shall not, therefore, be lacking in respect for Holy Scripture, for God's revelation of himself and of the realization of his eternal plan of love and salvation, if we identify in it a procedure to which the message of music bears some resemblance. In addition to its literal meaning, the Bible text has one or more spiritual meanings; or, if we follow a modern, more exact view, it presents something like the gradation of a single light: at first sensory and dimmed, it becomes as one advances in depth ever brighter, ever more immaterial and far-reaching in the splendor of its effulgence. The ancient Jews' Jerusalem, for example, the Zion that was at the heart of theocratic religion under David and Solomon, is first and foremost a type of Christ's Church, heir to the synagogue and realizer of the promises of Judaism. But in a deeper sense it prefigures the Christian soul, in which the mystery of the Church is alive in its entirety. Finally, the reality-type deepens and expands so as to signify the heavenly Jerusalem, that is, the company of elect souls perfected in glory, of whom Saint John in his Apocalypse gives us some idea. Thus we move from a material but already holy city to a city that is at once corporeal and divine. This in turn finds fulfilment beyond time and space, under the breath of the Spirit, in the eternal homeland of the elect established in the vision of God.

We can now turn again to music. Through combinations of sounds that first address our senses, we touch the heart of music only *beyond* certain realities susceptible of definition. Think of some work by Schumann or Debussy. It may at first evoke a landscape, a familiar vista, a more or less definite setting, a forest, a garden in the rain, a child playing or going to sleep, or a picturesque evening in Granada. Beneath the surface, however (though always in conjunction with it), the same music is suggesting a state of soul, the vibrations of a sensibility more or less ardent or discreet. It offers access to a more interior reality. Finally, beyond a halo of images and impressions, "at the end of everything," as Maurras would say, sovereign beauty arises. That is where we touch the ray of the eternal and divine which is the essential element of music, its definitive and indefinable reality. We are captivated by this sudden flash; in Scholastic terms, by a "fulguration of intelligence shining upon the proportionate parts of matter." It runs through the whole work as a sap of life. It bestows on every composition its proper value and makes of it an authentic creation. Because of it, there is more music in a single one of Schumann's *Kreisleriana* or *Kinderszenen* than in an entire opera by Massenet, or in a brief Bach chorale charged with mysticism than in the complete organ works, in themselves not uninteresting, of Pachelbel.

Anyone who has not been seized by this divine light has not yet gained access to music; he knows only its forecourts. In this perspective of an essential, divine element, it is quite true that music is "a construct of sound, nothing else." All our feelings have been exceeded. We stand before an absolute of truth and love shining forth in beauty. Whatever the modalities of its appearance, this absolute touches us beneath the surface of our soul. The pure beauty that transpires beyond the signs invites us to transcend music and go beyond ourselves in order to join it in its sanctuary.

We may draw one further parallel with Holy Scripture, which also speaks through signs and symbols. Even as the sacred text contains unveiled utterances that are endowed with a unique, purely spiritual meaning offering boundless perspectives (for example: "Before Abraham was, I am"; "God is love"), there are musical compositions so free of human alloy, so directly joined to their creative source that they effect our communion with the mystery of an invisible world without the mediation of definite thoughts or emotions. They are simply the ineffable song of supernatural light and tenderness. By stirring what is most secret in us, many such works at once enrich and purify our sensibility, which is touched but not exasperated by the sonorous signs, responding with a shock of emotion so deep that it defies analysis. I think of certain works by Bach or Mozart, like the beginning of that violin sonata in E-Minor to which I have already referred.

Mozart! Could anyone whose taste has not been corrupted by the artificial or falsely sublime, anyone whose heart has at least in its wellspring remained virginal, hear this song issuing from an exceptionally pure and loving soul without being moved to the point of bursting? A grace of innocence must have touched that soul unaffected by any concern to please, exteriorize, or astonish, aspiring only to sing. A few fugitive notes from a great broken chord falling back to their point of departure—and suddenly we are at the heart of music. We shall see later how, by virtue of its limpid message, this creation of a true genius of music breathes at once such happiness and such nostalgia.

However, let us be neither exclusive nor systematic. It matters little, after all, whether a more or less vague context of feelings and images envelops the pure essence of music, as long as we find it, as long as we present it with a soul that is open and ready to perceive its divine influence.

The *Kyrie eleison* and *Sanctus* from the Mass in B-Minor were made to carry a given text. The *Kyrie* evokes the universal aspect of a cry of supplication; the *Sanctus*, the immaterial undulations of angels in adoration. Have they for that reason less spiritual density than one of the same Bach's great Preludes and Fugues for organ, simple edifices of sound where there is only an elusive grandeur? When, even a long way away from an opera house, I look at the score of *Pelléas*, I can easily imagine the mysterious ambiance of sets and characters. Does it therefore have a less authentic musical value, for me, than Franck's symphony or his quartet, which evoke nothing definite? We *should* distinguish the popular repertoire from pure music, but it would be unjust to underestimate the former. Nor should we *a priori* condemn certain procedures that, by appealing to the imagination or sensibility of the listener or student, can occasion in him an awakening by which he is enabled to enter the depths of music.

In support of this assertion we may think of Cortot and the often suggestive commentaries with which he introduced performances of Chopin's twenty-four Preludes, the Preludes Schumann once described as "eagle's feathers." They seem, with their concentrated character of expression, the most sincere part of Chopin's works, the part most charged with pathos. "This piece," the Fourth Prelude, "must be played carrying a veil of mourning upon the face, with tears behind. . . . In the right hand, nothing but a groan, the groan of a being with no strength to raise its voice." On the Ninth: "Give the impression of a great curtain withdrawing to reveal, at the fortissimo, the victory of Samothrace, in full formation." On the marvelous Seventeenth: "The diction should be expressive enough to enable one to put a syllable under each note. At bar sixty-one, let the expression of your chords evoke an ideal embrace clutching some great happiness." And finally, on the dark, dramatic Prelude in C-Minor: "Show us a retreating funeral procession bearing away what is dearest to us, tearing it irrevocably from us."[10]

---

[10] I have likewise heard the great pianist Francis Planté use this procedure of suggestion by images and ideas. The Prelude in D-Minor from

It is self-evident that this kind of procedure, to be effective and not to risk vulgarizing music, must be exactly performed and used only with discretion. It is a matter of suggesting by awakening attention, nothing more. Any mere chatter in this area would be quite odious. Yet it cannot be denied that the approach, used discerningly, has pedagogical value. It can grant access to a depth where there is no longer any question of joy or sorrow or any precise image, but only the silent beauty which is at the root of all art. Here signs and symbols have finished playing their part and leave us enraptured in the pinnacle of our mind: the place of contemplation and love, the place of encounter with the essence of Beauty whose reverberation and resonances within us defy measurement.

♪ ♫ ♪

If the sonorous signs are *only* signs, that is, transmitters of a hidden reality, it is easy to understand that the way in which they are chosen and used reveals not only the composer's depth of inspiration but also the purity of his genius and intentions. At one extreme we find an extenuation of sound material that, on the pretext of spiritualizing music, is inclined to disregard the normal conditions of its action on the senses and to render it elusive; at the other extreme, there is a kind of intemperance, even debauchery, in the manner of manipulating the signs that is no less deadly. If combinations of rhythm, melody, and harmony are ruled by a concern to impress the listener, to do him a kind of violence, if they seek to

---

the Well-Tempered Clavier represented for him a procession of bishops moving with great pomp; the brisk Fugue in B-Flat Minor, the meeting of three drinking companions. The *andante* movement of Beethoven's Seventh Symphony, which he played impressively in Liszt's piano transcription, he called the March of Saints, etc. On this point, cf. Maritain, *Art*, 124f. The author stresses that the presence or outline of a concept, however vague, apt to suggest ideas, is in no way formally constitutive of the perception of beauty.

affect his nerves more than his soul, if they occur merely to fill a gap or to bring out the performer's virtuosity, then they do not answer to their value as signs: they become an end in themselves, at the service of a prostitution of art.

There are, alas, great geniuses who are not pure geniuses. Here I think of Wagner, of the pernicious commotion, the sonorous showiness that, in an overheated atmosphere of passion or false mysticism, bears a philter that can fetter us as magically as the one which bound Tristan to Isolde. Art of this kind forces emotion by stirring the troubled regions of our sensibility. It sublimates them without purifying them. At times, grace is needed to reject its pernicious charm. With Wagner, we are at the opposite extreme of Mozart and also of Bach, whose technical transports and most lively outbursts are always at the service of a truth that is authentic, healthy, and profound. They are bearers of an energy that does not crush the listener's heart but rather causes it to open out, that exalts without communicating any artificial intoxication to the dubious and superficial regions of our soul.

But between these two types—that of Bach and that of Wagner—what a more or less proportionate mixture of purity and impurity, sincerity and insincerity, true inspiration and simple craftsmanship we find even in true artists, notably in the "Romantics"! I do not think that Schubert, the transparent Schubert, whose soul, I would say, is akin to Mozart's, ever dabbled in falsehood, nor that incomparable artist, Schumann. But without speaking of Weber, Mendelssohn, or Liszt above all; did Chopin not cede more than once to the allurement of virtuosity? A simple ballad whose opening idea seduces us by its fresh simplicity can leave us disappointed when the initial theme gets excited to the point of carrying us away amid technical acrobatics into some kind of tormented dream.

Beyond Schumann, Mozart, Bach, and Palestrina, I suggest that we find the model purity of musical art most fully realized in the Gregorian cantilena of ages past. It is its prerogative to achieve the very highest, densest expression by minimal means.

Charged with incomparable spiritual truths, it never sets out to impress, it never seeks to excite our emotions. It is the voice of the Word, of the Spirit. The Spirit that regulates the Church's heartbeat is its quickening breath and, like the Spirit, Gregorian chant treats us with great respect: *cum magna reverentia*. It is not lacking in humanity, for it does respond to the demands of our senses. But it does so with such sobriety and penetration that we are led into the sphere of the most sacred realities. As we have already noted, Gregorian chant is a truly matchless music, steeped in grace and divine tenderness.

From the performer's point of view, too, the notion of music as "sign" is of great significance. What should be the object of one who has for his mission to perform a work in order to reveal it to himself and others, if not to deliver the signs of their spiritual content? For sure, it is a weighty enterprise to unravel this element of the eternal and divine, to enable it to blaze through signs that at once conceal and reveal it, to make it shine out by passing it on, for the joy and ennoblement of one's fellow human beings. To bring about such disclosure, to let it saturate one's being and then to pass it on, certain basic conditions must be met, apart from the technical mastery that ensures the material performance of any work.

First of all, perfect objectivity is called for. It is not the work that should adapt to us but we who should partake of its mystery and make it our own. To this attitude, we must add a susceptibility to beauty that, in order to be effective, requires self-emptying and a degree of purity to which the orientation of our being does not normally incline us. Beauty, as an object of contemplation, addresses that which is greatest and most profound in us, and we can say with Keats: "The most difficult, to keep heights which the soul is competent to gain." Finally, the spiritual content of a truly beautiful work is not generally delivered right away. It requires calm, slow, faithful, and silent familiarity. In order to harvest its riches and myriad nuances, we must invest patience and hard work, work that will perhaps never be finished.

At this point, it is fitting to say a word or two about attention, about the "attention" that is utterly different from "tension," being an attitude more passive than active, even if its immobility is more fruitful than all our agitation here below. Attention is like the gaze of a soul that, in order to receive, empties itself and waits. It has been well said: "Art is spontaneous like love, but it is cultivated like friendship." The beauty it lets us touch through sensory signs has manners, niceties, and depths (above all) of its own that can only be discovered little by little, on condition that we let ourselves be conquered and shaped by beauty. Beauty calls us. It makes demands that are certainly always agreeable but that may, if we attend to its voice, require sacrifices. Beauty's appeal to our heart, its influence over us, is such that we cannot treat it as if it were an abstraction, leaving us nothing but emptiness or fleeting consolation. We should not underestimate the graces of interiority available to a pianist, if he is truly an artist, in the solitary and recollected hours during which he works (while striving to listen in inward silence) on some great work that issues from beauty and develops, little by little, in the pure wake of beauty. I think, for example, of Opus 110, perhaps the most admirable of Beethoven's sonatas for its mournful serenity. It is the fruit of spiritual conquest and is crowned by a peace that surpasses every feeling. I think of some partita or toccata by Bach, marvels of invention and balance that invite endless meditation; of Schumann's wonderful Concerto in A-Minor; or of Franck's Prelude, Chorale, and Fugue, in which the religious imprint that marks any authentically beautiful work makes itself felt fully, for the work resembles, in Cortot's words, a long prayer brought to a close by a large sign of the cross. These are old works forever young that will never completely reveal their secret. Their language is as inexhaustible as the source from which they spring.

As Plato said of truth, we must come to beauty with all our soul. It is made to be contemplated by us, who were made for contemplation. How indeed could we resist its attraction as long as we have not found that other contemplation enjoyed by the perfect and by saints in the secret of God's kingdom? Who knows if on the human level, where in any case grace is never absent, the beauty of art may not direct us toward the supernatural horizons of which it is a foretaste? Even as it is a symbol of mystical contemplation, the contemplation of beauty has its own degrees and modalities. Most often, the beauty of a work of genius surrounds and penetrates us like the sea. We bathe in it, though without losing our foothold, without diving into the depth of its abyss. Rare, fleeting, and truly mysterious is the perception of beauty in its pure, luminous essence. It assails us like lightning. It imposes itself suddenly after the manner of some unexpected grace and projects us beyond self-awareness toward an unknown in which every fullness is contained.

I would appeal to a recent experience I myself had while playing a composition for organ by Nicolas de Grigny, a piece that is simple, majestic, and amazingly calm in its development. Suddenly, after a well-defined ascent, a long thetic movement ends in one of the composer's masterful appoggiaturas and opens onto an ineffable depth of adoration. It was as if a flash of lightning sprung from inaccessible light had pierced my night, leaving me dazzled and overwhelmed by such grandeur. When out of ecstasy I returned to myself, it seemed that this sudden immersion into the royal domain of beauty justified Simone Weil's remark: "[The] movement of descent, the mirror of grace, is the essence of all music. All the rest only serves to enshrine it. The rising of the notes is a purely sensorial rising. The descent is at the same time a sensorial descent and a spiritual rising. Here we have the paradise which every being longs for: where the slope of nature makes us rise towards the good."[11]

[11] *Gravity and Grace*, trans. Emma Craufurd (London: Routledge and Kegan Paul, 1952), 137.

It is beyond doubt that alongside our noblest aspirations music carries within itself the fundamental inclinations of our soul. And it is precisely on account of its expressive way of conveying our most intimate self that it constitutes, for those capable of understanding its language, an ever living, ever new source of emotion and delight. This aspect of its message will progressively impress itself on us as we attempt to unlock its mystery. Before closing this chapter, we may content ourselves with stating a fact of capital importance that flows naturally from our considerations so far: if music uncovers for us a spiritual reality that eludes our grasp beyond the signs it employs, beyond every idea and every feeling, it is because this reality is itself a sign and has the value of a sign.

♪ ♫ ♪

Here on earth, everything is a sign. Everything reveals an element of mystery that we must unravel, for the sign itself is a veil that hides what it covers but at the same time lets it show through in the process of transmission. Some Greek philosophers, Plato above all, and some ancient religions had an intuition of this truth. Plotinus, who brought their strands together so remarkably, considered the world an image of immaterial things, an image that never ceases to be formed: εἰκὼν ἀεὶ εἰκονιζόμενος [sic] (2 Enneads 3:18). It is the poet's prerogative to see nature as a vast universe of signs and to sense behind them a world of invisible realities. In Baudelaire's famous formulation:

> *Nature is a temple whose living pillars*
> *At times give voice to obscure words.*
> *Within it man passes through forests of symbols*
> *That watch him with a knowing look.*

Those who are brought by visible things to suspect an infinitely desired Beyond entertain the dream—the mad dream—to seize what they sense, in spite of the veil that keeps it from us. As Francis Thompson wrote:

O world invisible, we view thee,
O world intangible, we touch thee,
O world unknowable, we know thee,
Inapprehensible, we clutch thee!

What would our amazement be if all creatures here below would reveal to us their secret, from the countless chasms of incandescence that stud the universe of stars to the smallest grain of sand? We should undoubtedly be like the Bride of the Song of Songs, described by one of the greatest souls ever to contemplate her mystery as "struck to the heart by the beauty of things and pierced by the brilliance of their splendor as by a choice arrow, truly wounded and consumed by a blessed love."[12]

It is in this perspective, which places creation at the confines of two worlds, one visible, the other invisible, in a luminous center that envelops the totality of beings, that the contemplative recognizes a host of signs. He is situated on a supernatural plane irradiated with superior brightness. The signs thus perceived are to the contemplative so truly bearers of spiritual reality that he does not hesitate to consider nature, after the Bible, as a book that reveals divine and hidden things. "These two books," says Richard of Saint Victor, "produce the same sound, and harmonize to tell the wonders of a secret world." Nature and the Bible combine to uncover the presence of the First Cause that is humbly hidden behind created things, calling us with so many signs.[13] Both nature and Scripture indicate the presence of God, the One, of whom Louis

---

[12] [The translation follows the author's version, which takes some liberty with Origen's text, cited in a footnote:] *Ipsa rerum venustate percussus, et splendoris magnificentia ceu iaculo, ut ait propheta, electo terebratus, salutare ab ipso vulnus accipiet, et beato igne amoris eius ardebit* (*Commentary on the Song of Songs*, Prologue 17).

[13] At this point one could refer to several noteworthy testimonies in the works of Saint Bonaventure, Hugh of Saint Victor, and Cardinal de Cusa. Closer to ourselves, Cardinal Newman, influenced by the Alexandrian fathers and himself a poet gifted with remarkable intuition,

Massignon magnificently says that he is not an invention but a discovery. But what are they made from, these signs seen or heard, if not from states and vibrations of matter? "The totality of matter itself becomes a sign," said Michel Carrouges, "as soon as it becomes pervious to spirit by all its pores." Is there in our world any matter more pervious to the spirit than sound, the fundamental element of music, than the human voice of which it has justly been said that it springs forth from man as if by necessity, without any mediator other than itself? In the unity of the person, the voice is always united to the soul, always available to express its tenderest, most intimate motions. Further, may we not be permitted to think that music, among the prodigious constellation of signs that make up the universe, is particularly apt to lead us back to the source of life and beauty, particularly fit to function as a conduit toward the spiritual realm whose life in us, in God, and in the invisible world has its own rhythms, melodies, and harmonies? Is music not the sign that, more than any other, exercises overwhelming persuasive power over those able to hear its voice, delighting our senses in order to make them convey their message to the depths of the soul? Is it not, finally, the natural order's most revealing sign of a hidden God insofar as it implies a sovereign unity, the sovereign harmony of Being and of all beings in Being?

Hopefully our enquiry will shed some light on these issues by broadening and deepening our perspectives in the pursuit of mystery. If at this point we attempt to define our position, we find ourselves before a given fact, which is the imprecise language of music, saying nothing yet saying all; and before an experience, which is the perception of beauty and of the emotion it arouses. The experience implies a subject, which is our soul, and an object, which is beauty, the created beauty

---

developed perspectives on the invisible world as seen through the visible in a profound and pleasing way, above all in his sermons.

that, beyond the sign in which it is embodied, leads us to its uncreated source, the *secretissima* and *penetralia* of music, to the mysterious sanctuary we recognize as the ineffable, eternal, and divine reality in which all art originates and from which it acquires its worth.

Situating the Perception of Beauty

OUR ENQUIRY INTO THE MYSTERY OF MUSIC has disclosed to us, beyond the signs of sound, that divine, eternal element which is the deepest secret of art. It now confronts us with a further mystery: that of our soul. When we consider beauty in its dual (objective and subjective) aspect, we see it springing from a relation or harmony between some unknown world and our own inner world. We must now probe the latter.

There can be no doubt that the stirring yet pacifying emotion awakened in us by music affects an area that reaches a great deal deeper than our cold reason or our heart of flesh. Since beauty is of the intelligible order and infinitely lovable, we can take it for granted that its touch causes our faculties of knowing and loving to unfold in a kind of inebriation. Yet the fact that beauty does not generally engender any clear notion; the sudden, indefinable character of its hold on us; the impression of blissful plenitude with which it fills us; and finally, the liberation it effects by drawing us out beyond our limitations and banal selfishness, like a great gust of sea breeze instantly sweeping away our earthbound attachments: all these factors cause us to think that our soul contains unexplored depths attuned to an invisible reality for which music, like any art, is a "continuous desire" (Jules Laforgue).

How do we go about examining these depths? How can we attempt to define them? We are so limited! Only at moments of great revelation, when, far from the constant experience of our senses, we enter the sphere of eternity, do we see with faces unveiled, in the light of him who is Truth itself. As for here and now, what do we perceive of our soul except its superficial movements and sometimes disconcerting responses? And still, every profound soul, naturally inclined to what is right, has some foreboding (aided, no doubt, by a grace whose full impact cannot be measured) of its own depths, and desires to enter them. Some secret instinct alerts it to its original nobility; leads it to suspect that it bears something sacred in its innermost self.

Proclus, the pagan philosopher whose spiritual doctrine so amazed Tauler, discovered in himself a zone of silence which he called "a silent understanding unrelated to my senses, steeped in a kind of sleep—divine; a mysterious search, raised far above reason, for the One."[1] In our own day, another philosopher, but one marked by the most authentic Christianity, Louis Lavelle, concluded his book *The Dilemma of Narcissus* by describing what he calls the pinnacle of the soul or consciousness.[2] This pinnacle is, in Lavelle's opinion, a region of happiness which our thought and our will long to make their own and which, once we have touched it, we shall never want to leave. It is conceived of as a brilliant peak accessible only to the purest form of activity, where the soul attains its most perfect, and least enduring, equilibrium; or again, as an intention so simple and just that the world (seen, as it were, from within) responds to it with docility and fulfils it, so it seems, by the significance it receives; a region, finally, of a sovereign peace untroubled by what takes place in the soul's lower part. It is certainly not the "unconscious" of psychology that is at issue here but rather a supra-consciousness or a supra-temporal consciousness ill adapted to the clear-cut notions of practical

---

[1] Proclus was a neo-Platonist philosopher of the sixth century and a hierophant of the Eleusinian mysteries. His writings are marked by austere, deep spirituality; however, I do not presume to evaluate the degree of illumination that may have entered his mystical experience.

[2] *The Dilemma of Narcissus*, trans. William Gairdner (New York: Larson, 1993), 220f.

life and its circumstances. By it we enter into communion with the eternal and divine in a kind of silent passivity.

It seems to me that there are two classes of men fit to shed light on this depth of our spiritual being, since they alone may have had some experience of it, namely, the mystics and poets. Let us be careful not to confound them! Although the mystic may be a poet and the poet a mystic—and one could wish for no happier alliance—they are, as such, situated on two different planes. The mystics have been conformed, by charity, to God's nature; the poets have been conformed to the mysterious forces at work in the world. The former see themselves and all else in the light of him who has redeemed them and created them anew by grace; the latter see themselves in the brightness of him who, in an eternal present, creates them (within the totality of beings that, like himself, flow from the source of Being) and who continues through them his work of creation.

The mystic and poet are both inspired, the first by the Spirit who bestows the sevenfold gift and guides him back to the great current of trinitarian life; the second is inspired by the breath of God present in everything to which God gives being and life. God is free to dispense to man, in the natural order, what we call genius, even as he is, in the supernatural order, the origin of all holiness. By confronting the mystics' experience of touching God in their soul's sanctuary with the poets' intuition of Being and their own deepest self, we shall get a clearer sense of the abyss of interiority toward which music leads us, as a true ambassador, like all art, of divine beauty. We shall likewise recognize the place of such beauty in human experience. Would it not, then, be profitable to consider this double testimony?

♪ ♫ ♪

We turn first to the spiritual giants. Having pursued that science of the knowledge of God and self that is man's noblest activity, are they not like beacons in the night for us, their brethren? *Noverim me, noverim te* ["Let me know myself, let me know thee!"], exclaimed Saint Augustine after his conversion, in an excess of desire that was soothed only beyond death.[3] To such as these the mystery of man has been opened even in its most moving secrets, with that conjunction of misery and greatness so admirably echoed in Pascal.

The notion of *mens* as understood by Saint Augustine appears to underpin most things that have been thought and written about the depth of the soul—the soul God created with such a singular disposition of love that he made it with a deep sigh, as it were, as if drawing it out from his own heart.[4] In order to understand what this soul-depth is, we must pursue it back to the creative act by which being is bestowed in infinite kinds and degrees by him who, alone, is Being. "God sees in his Ideas every way in which his essence can be manifested and to their pattern he makes creatures, so setting the seal of his likeness over the whole range of creation, and detaching things from the life they had in him and in which they were he, only to find again in them a vestige of himself."[5]

To think that every creature should carry God's imprint and correspond to an eternal idea is already lovely, but it is lovelier still for man to be made in the image of the Creator by virtue of his free, immortal soul, for him to carry in his soul's depth the indelible impression of that image. It is precisely in the "silent, passive understanding" of which Proclus wrote, in Louis Lavelle's "summit of consciousness," in the "seed of eternity which even now catches breath beyond time" spoken of by Henri de Lubac (following Maritain) that the idea presiding over our creation is found to rest, living and luminous.

---

[3] *Soliloquia*, II.1.

[4] On the notion of *mens* in Saint Augustine and Saint Thomas, see Ambroise Gardeil, *La Structure de l'âme et l'expérience mystique*, 2 vols. (Paris: Gabalda, 1927), I, part 1.

[5] Maritain, *Art*, 70.

And so there is, over and beyond our faculties, at the point where they originate, a mysterious sanctuary where we are inseparably joined to God and maintained by him upon the abyss of void, posed as a living mirror of his life and being. In this mirror, beyond habitual consciousness, our interior gaze meets that of our Creator, outside the confines of space and time.

I cannot cite here the many admirable passages in which great contemplatives from Saint Augustine to our own day have spoken about this depth, this center or summit of the soul.[6] Sometimes they qualify it as a "living life" because it is in direct communion with him who is Life itself; sometimes

---

[6] Writers' choice of the terms "center" or "summit" depends on whether they consider the created order to be exterior or inferior to this pure region. "Depth," on the other hand, implies a hidden, impenetrable reality. In no way do I presume, here, to expound a thorough teaching on the notion of the soul's "depth." It has been treated by theologians from Saint Augustine and Saint Thomas to Fathers Gardeil and Théry (as in their introduction to Tauler's sermons) with all the discrimination due to so delicate a question. We should remember, however, that what is at issue is a reality that, for its spiritual depth and elusive nature, has no foothold in the order of created things: the vocabulary commonly applied to it was not made for it and can only suggest, not define. In the present text, I shall state only what is necessary for an understanding of our subject, while indicating a few sources: Saint Augustine and his commentators; William of Saint-Thierry (especially in his remarkable treatise *De natura et dignitate amoris*); Saint Bonaventure, also a disciple of Augustine; and above all the great German and Flemish mystics such as Ruusbroec in his various treatises, Henry Suso, and Tauler, in whose sermons the depth of the soul recurs as a kind of leitmotif. François-Louis de Blois (Blosius), abbot of Liessies, presents a confluence of the Rhenish-Flemish school and summarizes their teaching toward the end of his *Institution spirituelle*, an admirable treatise much savored by Francis de Sales. Closer to ourselves are the two great Spanish mystics of Carmel. Nor should we forget the Venerable Jean de Saint-Samson, who pioneered the reform of Carmel in France. Closer still is Père Rabussier. His beautiful texts on the *Oraison du mariage spirituel* were collected by Madame Cécile Bruyère, abbess of Sainte-Cécile de Solesmes. Long unpub-

as a "passivity" that is also supreme activity insofar as it touches him who is pure Act (for it is when the soul has consciously attained this center that it acts most powerfully upon God and the world); sometimes as a "pinpoint" representing the extremity of our being both in the order of our origin and in that of our return toward God. It is, then, the region of perfect simplicity and unity, the place where grace is born and finds fulfillment. Here is the true homeland we are called to recover through an ascent in depth toward our original being and through an outpouring of grace that divinizes our faculties of knowing and loving, leading them back by a kind of reflux in our innermost self toward the Father. For the Father made us by his Word and by his Spirit of love only so as to lead us back, by them, to his unfathomable unity.[7]

Here we find repose. Here we find a life that, as a prelude to the life of paradise, bestows unassailable blessing. It is a solitude charged with an overwhelming presence that no one can find except in the *interiora deserti* ["deepest parts of the desert"] that Scripture speaks of (Exod 3:1), that is, at the very heart of the desert. Here indeed is the kingdom of God, where everything is naked, stripped, yet where infinite riches are found. For in this place extremes meet and mingle in perfect harmony; abyssal nothingness and void meet the wellspring and plenitude of being.

This place has further been named "heaven of the mind" or "spark of flame" by virtue of the irresistible propensity that, in it, attracts us to God while nonetheless keeping us, with

---

lished, they have now appeared in Joseph de Guibert's *Dictionnaire de spiritualité ascétique et mystique*.

[7] "Let yourself flow into that great All which is God so that you are nothing except in him. You were with him before the beginning of time, in his eternal decree; you sprang from him, so to speak, when his love drew you out of nothing. Return to this idea, to this decree, to this beginning, to this love." These are Bossuet's words in his fifty-fourth letter to Sœur Corneau.

him, at rest. Others have called it "memory." Man's life, like that of the triune God in whose image he is created, is intelligence and will, and his memory—source of the faculties of knowing and loving—bears a correspondence to the Father, who, hidden in the impenetrable silence of the Godhead, expresses himself *ad intra* as well as *ad extra* only by his Word and Spirit. The notion of memory here acquires singular density.

Even in the sense we ordinarily give it, memory is rather a mysterious faculty. We appreciate how its unforeseeable workings could fill Saint Augustine's soul with wonder. Only think of those passages in the *Confessions* where the author with accustomed perspicacity attempts to explore this vast palace (*lata praetoria*), this impenetrable, limitless sanctuary (*penetrale amplum et infinitum*). He does not manage to reach its innermost recesses and can only refer with a kind of dread to the deep and boundless multiplicity (*nescio quid horrendum profunda et infinita multiplicitas*) of this immeasurable capacity whose force is very great (*magna ista vis*).[8]

Yet even if its content and operation are inscrutable, this same memory, which is both sensitive and intelligent, somehow remains submitted to our consciousness. Saint Augustine, in expounding the notion, asserts that the memory we carry in us is "the ability at any moment to recover within ourselves the hidden presence of God, especially of his goodness and power." As he puts it in a happy turn of phrase: God is always with us, even if we are not always with him. Étienne Gilson, who studied the influence of Augustine's thought on the Middle Ages, put it like this:

> At the summit of the mind therefore there is a secret point where resides the latent remembrance of [God's] goodness and his power; and there also lies the most deeply graven trait of his image, that which evokes all the others and

[8] *Confessions*, X.8, 17.

enables us to make ourselves like him. In God, the Father generates the Son, and from the Father and the Son proceeds the Holy Spirit. In us in the same way, immediately and without any interval of time, memory generates reason and from memory and reason proceeds the will. The memory possesses and contains in itself the term to which man should tend; reason at once knows that we ought so to tend; the will tends; and these three faculties make up a kind of unity but three efficacies, just as in the Divine Trinity there is only one substance but three Persons.

Basing himself on an admirable text by William of Saint-Thierry (*Memoria quippe habet et continet quo tendendum sit; ratio, quod tendendum sit; voluntas tendit*),[9] the same author goes on to add:

Here then we have the thing that God created; here also therefore we see what is man's "natural" state: that of a reason that knows naught but God, of a will that tends to naught but God, because the memory whence they proceed is filled with nothing but the remembrance of God. Such also was the divine image in man when it shone out in all its splendor, before it had been tarnished by sin.[10]

It is precisely to this "quo" that the saints have returned; to this sanctuary of memory where lies hidden, undamaged by the rust of sin, the pure image whose living reflection we are in our innermost reality. Following a lovely expression from Saint Gregory Nazianzen, the saints have restored to the Image (the Word) the beauty of the image: ἀποδῶμεν τῇ εἰκόνι τὸ κατ'εἰκόνα ["let us give back to the Image what is according to the Image"].[11] They have done so by remaining faithful to an ever unfolding grace that ultimately sets them down on

---

[9] *De natura et dignitate amoris* II.3.

[10] Étienne Gilson, *The Mystical Theology of Saint Bernard*, trans. A. H. C. Downes (London: Sheed & Ward, 1940), 204f.

[11] *Oratio* I.4.

the threshold of the end point where faith will turn to vision, where they may say with Saint John of the Cross to him who is their only love: "Tear the veil of this sweet encounter!" Through time and through suffering, by passing through the narrow gate, they have reached eternal joy. Their soul opens onto the infinity of God. Through a succession of nights, they have plunged ever more deeply into the light. Letting themselves be fashioned by the hand of him who is closer to them than their own self,[12] these supremely obedient souls have gained access to the sovereign freedom of love. They have truly become a new creation, living utterly the life of Jesus Christ, for whom they have come to constitute, as it were, an additional human nature.

By the ascent of their "I" to their "self," finally, the saints have laid hold of their true personality. For it seems clear that our true self is found in this mysterious sanctuary rather than in particularities of temperament owing to contingencies of race, family, social environment, and education. This is where we truly become a "person": a reality that is inimitable and unique because it corresponds to a unique idea on the part of God, because it is founded on a unique relation between us and God, and because, in it, the being bestowed on us reaches fulfillment. In this deep center we shall find inscribed the "new name" which is known only to the one who receives it (Apoc 2:17), a hidden name designating divine intimacy carried to its highest degree. It is in order to make it our own that we were created anew in the blood of Jesus. It is the name of the child who, on coming into Christ's maturity, has acquired his full inheritance of grace and assumed his place within the royal lineage of the Consubstantial Three.

The mystery of the soul, then, has led us to the intimate reality of our true self, where all is light, peace, order, joy, and

---

[12] *Interior intimo meo et superior summo meo* (Augustine, *Confessions* III.6).

tenderness. While with the Venerable Blosius we may deplore the fact that so many (even spiritual) people lack the courage to climb the solitary, naked peaks that touch this center and, what is more, that so many do not even know it exists, we understand that life's meaning is found in our return to this place of delights, where, for as long as we await the eternal encounter face-to-face, we shall enjoy, with the possession of our true and lasting self, the only truth, the only love, and the only presence that matter.

I have just referred to this region as a center. As such, it is also an accurate and spacious lookout post, surveying the entire created universe. How can that be? At this depth, where we enter into God, we likewise enter into his creative action. From here, we see all created things in him who is their efficient, exemplary, and final cause. The enraptured contemplation of the mind gives rise to an immense solidarity. The contemplative saint sees himself as a brother to all creatures, for they, like he, spring from abyssal void by the working of an infinite, all-powerful goodness that supports and embraces us all.

It is by the degree of their affinity to this perspective, which is a gift of Wisdom, as well as by their sense of an indefinable Beyond where the soul is rooted in the mystery of being, that the poets' experience presents an analogy to that of the mystics, similarly leading us back toward the transcendent zone of invisible realities. That is why, when the poet shares what inspiration's touch has revealed to him in his soul, now become a center of vision, we experience a thrill as before the revelation of an unknown world attuned to our most secret aspirations.

♪ ♫ ♪

O reserved, inspiring portion,
O reserved portion of myself!
O innermost part of me!
O thought of myself that was before I was!

> *O part of myself that are a stranger to every place*
> *And my eternal resemblance,*
> *Touching on certain night.*

Thus Claudel expresses himself in a few quivering lines that give voice to a priceless discovery.[13] At issue, but now on the natural plane, is the sacred depth we have just been discussing. The poet, too, touches it, and from this contact he grasps the Why? of his vocation. He places himself within it to authenticate his creative vein and justify his mission. Here is another equally moving testimony from Thomas Traherne:

> *My naked simple Life was I;*
> > *That Act so strongly shin'd*
> *Upon the Earth, the Sea, and Sky,*
> *It was the substance of the Mind;*
> > *The sense itself was I.*
> *I felt no dross nor matter in my Soul,*
> *No brims nor borders, such as in a bowl*
> *We see. My Essence was Capacity,*
> > *That felt all things.*

In this simple act, at this height where he is master of himself in the limpid clarity of an immense perspective, the poet's contemplation of things from within shines forth. He seeks to communicate the experience:

> *This made me present evermore*
> > *With whatsoe'er I saw.*
> *An object, if it were before*
> *My eye, was by Dame Nature's Law*
> > *Within my Soul. Her store*
> *Was all at once within me; all Her treasures*

---

[13] This and the following cited texts come from two remarkable articles by Marcel de Corte on which the present section is based. See "Ontologie de la poésie (I)," *Revue Thomiste* 43 (1937): 361–92; "Ontologie de la poésie (II)," *Revue Thomiste* 44 (1938): 99–123.

Were my immediate and internal pleasures,
Substantial joys, which did inform the Mind.
With all She wrought
  My Soul was fraught,
And every object in my Heart a Thought
    Begot, or was; I could not tell,
    Whether the things did there
        Themselves appear,
Which in my Spirit truly seem'd to dwell;
  Or whether my conforming Mind
  Were not even all that therein shin'd. . . .

A strange extended Orb of Joy,
  Proceeding from within,
Which did on every side convey
Itself, and being nigh of kin
  To God did every way
Dilate itself even in an instant, and
Like an indivisible Centre stand,
At once surrounding all Eternity.

Eternity! Yes, eternity itself is recovered, as Rimbaud likewise ascertains, and it is eternity that the poet must project onto earth: "If you can," said Carlyle, "discern a work of art from an artificial work, you will see eternity beholding, through time, the divine made visible." The poet touches it in his innermost being, and Traherne concludes:

O living Orb of Sight!
Thou which within me art, yet me!

Finding eternity, the poet wondrously finds his own self. In this unity and harmony—within the interior, spiritual sensibility where he is ineffably situated "upon the very pulse of being" (Claudel)—the poet, far from dissolving into what coexists with him and is at one with him, discovers his own personality. His self, his true self is in the "luminous consciousness of the whole" (Hugo von Hofmannsthal) that he encounters. But if he finds a way back to himself in all things, it is only because he has always been with all things, enveloped with them in the presence of him in whom all things live eternally and whom all things are appointed to speak and indicate according to their degree and mode of participation in Being.

The sublime aspect of the poet's vocation resides in his encounter with the invisible reality that transfigures all creation. Herein lies his gift to all humanity. With William Blake he can say:

> *I rest not from my great task!*
> *To open the eternal worlds,*
> *To open the immortal eyes*
> *Of man inwards into the worlds of thought,*
> *Into eternity.*

He who sees all things in the unity of what is eternal, who sees the flow of time coexist with what simply remains, has every reason to burst into joy.

> *The leaf fades. The fruit falls.*
> *Yet in my verse the leaf abides*
> *Along with the ripe fruit*
> *And the rose among roses.*
> *It perishes,*
> *But its name, in that mind which is my mind,*
> *Perishes not.*

A unity of this kind transcends time, as Claudel would have it:

> *Laugh, immortal, as you find yourself among*
>   *perishable things!*
> *Jeer, and see what once you took in earnest,*
> *Things that pretend to remain, yet pass;*
> *Things that pretend to pass, yet do not cease to be;*
> *While you yourself for ever are with God!*

In this way the poet redeems time. All the fugitive things that, with him, flow forth from eternity are brought back, by him, to eternity. Such is his mission. Such is his joy. His joy, no doubt, is profound, but so is his pain, especially if he belongs among the "poets of the night"[14] who, far removed from the certainty of faith, have no knowledge of the invisible, eternal secret they nonetheless touch with wonderful intuition.

Such a poet finds himself before a gaping mystery, more gripping than the stellar space whose silent infinity filled Pascal's soul with fear. But he cannot enter it. He touches a reality that attracts him forcefully, but cannot plunge into, cannot grasp its secret. In his deepest self is a strange solidarity with Being and all things that are, but the experience is dark and fleeting. He is unable to pin down the mystery whose revealing alone makes life worth living. He balances, in a kind of vertigo, between an abyss of greatness and an abyss of despair. We can easily see how this experience of an eternal and divine reality differs from that of the mystic who, upon recovering his true self in the love of Christ, "with eyes wide open to the deifying light,"[15] touches the mystery of his God in that "night without darkness" of which the Psalmist sings (Ps 138).

♩ ♫ ♩

The reader may think that these reflections have taken us far from the mystery of music. But no! We are at its heart. For what is this sovereign music if not the most intoxicating, the most spiritual poetry, apt to express, by its play on symbols of sound, the mystery of an unknown world, to sound that interior, divine silence which is at the root of all art and which rises from it? It is the prerogative of music to realize fully what pure poetry strives hopelessly to attain, for it is the language of the ineffable, of that which words cannot encompass.

---

[14] The expression is Claudel's and encompasses, among others, Poe, Mallarmé, Baudelaire, and Rilke.
[15] *Rule of Saint Benedict*, Prol. 9.

If, in order to discover the secret core of the soul from which true inspiration springs, appeal has been made to the poet's experience and testimony, it is because he speaks with words, that is, with signs corresponding to the demands of our intellect. It is by *thinking* that we first grasp what he says or suggests, whatever the magic force of evocation his genius uses to pour new sap into familiar terms. The musician, on the other hand, surrenders the secret of his inspiration in a language that eludes conceptual precision and throws us forthwith into the unknown.[16]

We have here to establish something of first importance. Even if we are not great mystics, even if we are middling and without genius, we too, like the saint, like the musician or poet, carry in our innermost being (even if we live too superficially to be conscious of it) that hidden sanctuary of memory where our faculties are rooted—that living mirror of God, that blazing spark, that silent and divine understanding, that reserved portion foreign to every time and place, that living orb which is, at our core, our true self, knit together in an embrace of solidarity with everything that, like us, flows from the source of Being. If it were not thus, how could sovereign music find in us so many resonances at once forceful and discreet? Under the fleeting touch of beauty, an awakening is wrought in us, the fruit of a freeing force that alerts us to our depths. Like every art, but with a penetration apparently unequalled, music is, "in some measure and at certain moments, the force which shatters the vault within which we suffocate."[17]

---

[16] We should note that painting and sculpture, like poetry, tear us less radically than music from the exterior world. While these forms of art may radiate something of the invisible, they leave us in a familiar framework of lines, forms, colors, and words.

[17] Ernest Hello, *L'Homme* (Paris: [n.pub.], 1872; repr. Éditions de Paris, 2005), 263f. The author goes on to develop a line of thought that is profound and true, even though his language is rather bombastic: "Poor fugitive notes, poor syllables carried off by the wind, invisible majesties:

Whether developed in a zone of intimacy (like a melody by Fauré or Duparc) or endowed with the cosmic character of a gigantic symphony, every true masterpiece draws us, if we can hear its message, out of the oblivion where we are kept in chains by a certain *fascinatio nugacitatis* ["enthrallment by the trifling"] and by a twofold poverty: the poverty of our intellect which, although made to embrace all and yearning to know the essence of things, proceeds only by successive reasoning and therefore remains so very limited in both the exercise and the result of its investigations; and the poverty of our heart, shrunk through selfishness, inattentive to our will's tendency to expand toward boundless love. Beauty carries with it, from expanses immense and eternal, a torrent of life.

♪ ♫ ♪

If music really reveals our true dimensions, it is a grave and serious matter. When it comes to us with its marvelously seductive power and its wholesome, pure beauty, we should receive it with respect, prepared, as it were, for a message from beyond the created world. We should receive it, too, with great spiritual delight. There are works of music that, for the density of their spiritual content, we should not hear too often. Were it not a kind of profanation to lack temperance in their

---

How powerless you are! You stir the earth. The heavens hear you. In those solemn moments when we are yours, our soul is filled with oxygen. It breathes and awakens to itself: 'I am great, O my God, but had forgotten my greatness.' Through you, the human soul tastes the first-fruits of its deliverance, amazed at its customary forgetfulness, amazed that it does not always remember what in an instant it recalls. An accidental light reveals the depth of usual darkness. The soul's understanding is absorbed by the awakening. It thinks of its slumber with astonishment. . . . A thick and heavy gate, our prison gate, conceals our great love."

regard? Does not beauty, carrier of grace, demand to find us at its own level? It comes to us as sovereign.[18]

Perhaps we shall gain a more precise understanding of the sacred character of works of genius if we think not only of ourselves but of those whose mission it is to convey, through art, the voices of invisible worlds, for this transmission generally requires of the artist, who is a creature of flesh and blood, a passage through sacrifice and pain. How could it be otherwise? If the gift of genius implies an inspiration from our Creator God, if it assimilates man to the secret powers of the universe, if it entails an opening onto eternity, then the one who receives it is subject to a veritable distension that cannot be without suffering. In the words of Gustave Thibon, "the man of genius is at once profoundly one with the world and profoundly cut off from the world. His genius is born of communion and isolation, and of the tearing apart that ensues. A work of genius is communion reflected and eternalized by isolation; it is the world rediscovered, re-created, in the mirror of Narcissus."[19]

Furthermore, a great work of art does not always spring from joyful spontaneity. Sometimes it is brought to birth through much pain. We do not think in these terms when we hear it, any more than we wonder, upon seeing a handsome child, whether its mother suffered much and long in bringing it into the world. Beauty is there. That is enough. But short of exceptional assistance, it cannot be a slight matter to carry on God's own creative work, to offer him without betrayal a conduit that will always remain imperfect, to attune the soul's

---

[18] We should note that music can, without demeaning itself, provide us with refreshment and repose. As long as its source remains pure and healthy, light, attractive music betrays neither its role nor its nobility. Mozart's *Rondo alla turca*, Ravel's *Conte de ma mère l'Oye*, Debussy's *Danse de Puck*, although they do not belong to the highest spheres of music, are all imbued with beneficent charm.

[19] *Le Pain de chaque jour* (Monaco: Du Rocher, 1945), 125.

supraconscious depths to the vibrations of our human sensibility, to that play of our conscious faculties which occupies a large part in the elaboration and realization of a work of art. It is a hard thing to reconcile the demands of sincerity—a striving to be absolutely faithful to the creative impulse—with the demands of beauty expressed on the material plane. The task of working out the balance and harmony required for the structural perfection of a work must often be a source of labor and perpetual dissatisfaction.[20] To this we may add the rift wrought by two equally imperious instincts: the desire, experienced as necessity, to let a work express what one carries in oneself ("What is in my heart," said Beethoven, "must out") and the modesty which cringes at the thought of exteriorization, of passing on to all and sundry what is most intimately sacred to oneself.

Nor should we forget that music of the kind that speaks to us of the eternal and infinite, which links us with a love surpassing every other love, has time and time again had to clear its path through the most shattering trials of the human condition. Often it is written with blood. Look at Bach, apparently so objective and serene. Is it a mistake to seek in the repeated grief that pierced his loving heart the origin of that poignant sadness which inspired certain Cantatas, certain Chorales and the sublime pages of the Passions, where communion with the sufferings of the crucified Christ is perhaps not void of human resonances?[21] And what about Beethoven? Would he have reached the summits of the Fifth, Seventh, and Ninth

---

[20] We know, for instance, on Georges Sand's testimony, the agony Chopin went through in chiseling his Preludes, often in vain, as it happens. After many efforts, he would discover that their most perfect form was contained in the first outburst of inspiration.

[21] We know that Bach, an excellent husband and father, experienced the pain of losing his first wife in especially trying circumstances (while he was absent), and that, of the twenty-one children he had from two marriages, only eight were still alive at his death.

Symphonies or the last Piano Sonatas had he not known the sorrow and dereliction of loneliness, incomprehension, and illness? For him as for many others, suffering, sometimes terrible suffering, was the winepress from which the heart's greatness flowed forth in pure, heartrending beauty. The one love that is beyond every earthly love found in beauty its outlet, its way, its expression.

We can say of the musician what Léon Bloy said of the poet, that he is "a vessel of suffering." It is by passing through this crucible that the artist accomplishes his work of "re-creation" (a wonderful symbol of the work of grace) and exercises his true function, which, in the words of Pope Pius XII, is "to break open the narrow and painful circle of finitude in which, here below, man is enclosed, and to provide a window for his mind aspiring to the infinite."[22] In this marvelous opening onto the eternal wellsprings of Being where, even in the midst of human pain, all is light, love, innocence, and joy, the visible world and the world of humble everyday realities are transfigured by a ray of invisible light. The visible world is charged with the solemnity and gladness of a birth ever present and virginal. Our everyday experiences are invested, under their veil of simplicity, with otherworldly, mysterious greatness.

Art cannot bestow God, but it points to him from whom it springs. It would make us cling to him, were we not bogged down in sin or numbed by superficiality. By whatever signs it may appear, every manifestation of created beauty is like that window in the Song of Songs by which the Lover is separated from his Beloved. Through the trelliswork, the Lover sees without being seen. He waits. He does not want to reveal fully that he is there. He wants the soul's desire, so often in rebellion against the purely interior call of his grace, to know in advance of his coming. He wants the heart to sense him

---

[22] Allocution on sacred art to the Sixth Roman Quadriennale on 8 April 1952.

before the eyes can see. There is, naturally, a long way from this discreet intervention of God through created beauty, even at its most immaterial, to that of Christ who, having conquered the world, knocks on the door and asks to enter to consummate his union with the soul in the intimacy of a dazzling feast (Apoc 3:20). Yet it is the same God who comes, his head still moist with the dew of the night, while the Beloved is still not quite awake, and who appears resplendent with glory after vanquishing sin and death in order to lead his spouse into the stores of divine sustenance.

The Creator God and the Redeemer God are one. He is himself the Poet and very Poetry, the Musician and very Music. He is at once supreme Beauty and the Art of an all-powerful God, without whom there could be neither art nor beauty here below. He it is who, because he is love, desires to lead us into the joy which is his own joy, a joy of which music, to one who has ears to hear, perhaps gives the most wonderful foreboding of all. "Yes," wrote Claudel to Gabriel Frizeau, "believe this firmly, with unshakable assurance: there is no truth except in that immense, overwhelming, blessed joy of which the most sublime works of art—Virgil, Dante, Beethoven, Shakespeare— give us some small notion; everything that confirms us in this notion is true, everything that distances us from it is false. There can be no doubt that we are born for boundless happiness, for delights that words cannot express."

Music, Relation, and Tears

IT MAY BE WORTHWHILE to pause over a phenomenon that sheds light on the interior *locus* of our perception of beauty and on the spiritual depths touched by music's deep mystery. I refer to the tears that are sometimes brought spontaneously to our eyes by the shock of aesthetic emotion. Our tears: Do we ever reflect on what they signify when they are more than simply the effect of our exasperated sensibility, of an upheaval suffered by our heart of flesh? Where lies the source of our tears? Why do they seem to us almost sacred when they are tears of wonder, born, not of enthusiasm, but of a recollection that borders on adoration?

In order to understand the nobility of such tears and to deliver them of their secret, we might compare them to their contrary phenomenon: laughter. Laughter, and what strikes us as ridiculous, is the effect of disproportion, of rupture. A child affecting the mannerisms of a grown man; the observation of Hugo's urchin in *Les Misérables*, who, on seeing a dog so skinny that its bones seem to pierce its skin, exclaims, "Poor doggie, have you then swallowed a barrel?": these make us laugh. Laughter often points to a superficial view of things and people. The odd behavior of a drunkard or madman, which causes sadness in a serious, reflective mind, makes a light-minded onlooker laugh. As Ernest Hello justly remarks, a thing can make us laugh because it shatters relation and unites incommensurable ideas or phenomena. Relation, on the other hand, the intimate and profound relation which, once felt, calls (unlike laughter) for the soul's penetrating attention, is the mother of tears.[1]

Beauty springs precisely from such relation. It stirs our emotions in their most sacred, most hidden potential. When, in the unutterable tenderness of a boundless love, this relation unites things that are in themselves quite dissimilar, beauty reaches its peak and becomes sublime. Thus it is that the mystery of an all-powerful God making himself an infant in a hidden corner of our minuscule planet, then dying in a paroxysm of humiliation and pain in order to make us, poor sinners, gods and to re-create all things in an immensity of forgiveness and mercy: *this* is the supreme mystery of relation, before which our fountain of tears ought never to dry out.

But is it not everywhere present, this relation which constitutes the secret beauty of things and is sensed by the artist's inspiration? It produces the laws of universal rhythm that forever govern the life of men in a movement carrying all things to their proper end. It informs the phenomena of attraction and repulsion that, in mind-boggling harmony, guide the myriad suns and planets of our stellar universe. It is found here on earth, unfolding little by little, through time and space, in what Saint Augustine calls "the wonderful song of passing things"—in the poem of human history where every syllable is spoken, in relation to the ones that precede and follow it, with the quantity, pitch, nuance, and stress proper to itself.[2] It is evident in all beings that are commissioned to signify their Creator in an admirable hierarchy and progression, from the angels to the smallest grain of sand. By their multiplicity and variety, all contribute to the wealth and perfection of the cosmos. A similar relation is no less present in

---

[1] *L'Homme*, 53ff.

[2] Recalling the LXX rendition of Isaiah, in which God *profert numerose saeculum*, Augustine speaks of God's art *in hoc labentium rerum tamquam mirabilis cantico* (*Letter* 166.XIII). Cf. *Letter* 138.

human love, in the vital exchanges that enhance one being with the life of another. It meets us in the fluctuations of desire and peace, effort and rest, hope and possession that continually make up the fabric of our lives. It is, finally and above all, what unites us with him who has created us, or, rather, who creates us at each moment from his unchanging eternity—with God.

But who *is* God? Is he an abstraction, a blind and distant force, a perfection that remains closed, in inexorable transcendence, to everything that is not itself? No. We have seen that God is presence, a presence so universal, so real that he is closer to us than we are to ourselves. And if he is closer to us than we are to ourselves, then he is necessarily closer to us than any creature. For God, "that immense and boundless ocean" in the words of Gregory Nazianzen, God, who holds us in his creative hand, is "person." He is "person" to a degree that our existential notion of that concept cannot possibly encompass. He is so utterly "person" that the relations constituted by his single act of knowledge and love make him Person thrice over—Father, Word-Son, and Holy Spirit—in the inviolable and generative unity of his essence.

In the all-holy relations that unfold within the life of the Deity we must seek the cause and exemplar of every relation here below. They allow us to understand the sacred character of that fundamental relation which contains the rhythms of the universe in their solemn movement back to their Creator. At the risk of appearing to digress by speaking, here, of music (which nonetheless remains the subject we never lose sight of), we may note that relation somehow becomes incarnate in music, whose signs are all relative. Successive relations in intervals preside over melody's lines and rhythm's alternating momentum and rest. Simultaneous relation unites the multiple voices of harmony. The element of relation is the ordering principle of sound material. It brings tidings of an infinitely higher relation, thanks to the lightning flash of intelligence, to the splendor of form which essentially constitutes Beauty and sheds its radiance on the proportionate parts of matter.[3]

♪ ♫ ♪

Let us go one step further. I said a moment ago that we are united to God in relation. To say as much is to say not enough. We *are*, in truth, a living relation to God. "You have made us for yourself!" exclaimed Saint Augustine. Relation, and relation alone, gives meaning to our life, our being. To touch God in our soul's sanctuary by contact with the beautiful which is a manifestation of, a call from, the ocean of essence that is God, is a grace fully attuned to our deepest vocation: the call to be united to God in relation. It rightly fills us with pure, satiating joy, and it is this joy which brings tears to our eyes, tears that flow from a hidden, supraconscious source whose vibrations touch our sensibility. Such tears are rare and discreet, for they spring from a great depth, a depth that, when it rises briefly, affects the surface of our soul with the utmost tenderness. Here we find the one presence, the one love that can bring fulfillment. Our frontiers fade. For an instant we are conformed to an Immensity that opens us to itself, to an Eternity that beckons to us beyond the patchwork of appearances, to a Permanence that calls us through things transient and mortal. Everything vanishes before this deepening, this transcending of ourselves. It lets us taste the mystery of an immense world made of greatness and love, where, in all-embracing relation to God, we find solidarity with all that exists and is related to him.

---

[3] Saint Thomas, of course, attaches three conditions to the beautiful: integrity, because the mind loves that which is; proportion, because the mind loves order and unity; and brightness or clarity, because the mind loves light and intelligibility (*Summa theologiae* Ia.39, 8). Cf. Maritain, *Art*, 20.

Yet the tears that reveal the secret of our only love are not solely tears of happiness. They are complex tears, which also convey the most piercing nostalgia. How can that be? We must remember this: If, by virtue of our vocation and destiny as children of God, we are great, we have nonetheless, by sin, fallen from our first splendor. We are exiled from the Eden of joy and divine intimacy that was the lot of man in his innocence. Does there not remain in the heart of man a yawning void parched with thirst for this paradise lost? Beyond the thick forgetfulness that absorbs us, we carry within us the unforgettable call of a voice that echoes in invincible sadness. That call of the night makes us recognize an element of truth in the Platonic myth of remembrance, according to which we have fallen into a kind of slumber, after first enjoying an ideal world of light and love. Thus, Wordsworth sings:

> *Our birth is but a sleep and a forgetting:*
> *The Soul that rises with us, our life's Star,*
> *Hath had elsewhere its setting,*
> *And cometh from afar:*
> *Nor in entire forgetfulness,*
> *And not in utter nakedness,*
> *But trailing clouds of glory do we come*
> *From God, who is our home.*

We are brought to think of Saint Hildegard, the great musician to whom prophetic light revealed many secrets of nature and grace. She maintained that, while our soul has fallen from its first beauty, it remains possessed of harmony and retains the gift to express it. It is precisely when, under the breath of inspiration, the soul remembers that it is exiled far from Home (the condition of paradise) that it is able to communicate what vibrates and sings within it.[4] The memory of a paradise lost

---

[4] *Sed et anima hominis symphoniam in se habet et symphonizans est, unde etiam multotiens planctus educit, cum symphoniam audit, quoniam de patria in exilium se missam meminit. (Liber Vitae meritorum IV.46.)*

is thus at the root of both music and poetry. In the tears provoked by truly beautiful music we see perfect happiness
linked to great sorrow. There is nothing romantic, nothing
flatly sentimental in this impression of nostalgia, which is as
profound as the joy of relation restored is certain and
intoxicating.

Yet there is a paradise other than the Eden from which we
are forever banished, not an earthly paradise, but a heavenly
one of grace and glory opened for us by our God dying on a
cross. It is infinitely more beautiful than the first. Perhaps
without being conscious of the fact, it is principally for this
paradise we yearn, since for it we were created. Of course, it
is to this paradise that Baudelaire alludes when he speaks of
tears sprung from the shock of beauty as the expression of
"our inability to grasp *now*, wholly here on earth, at once and
for ever, those divine and rapturous joys of which *through* the
poem, or *through* the music, we attain to but brief and inde-
terminate glimpses." Rather than an excess of pleasure, such
tears "attest an irritation of melancholy, some peremptory
need of the nerves, a nature exiled in the imperfect which
would fain possess immediately, even on this earth, a paradise
revealed."[5] And are we not well aware that we shall, when
no longer drunk with the sweetness of our rapture, be brought
back to our usual limits, to be more or less stuck in what is
sensible and carnal?

These two poles—on the one hand, satiation, on the other,
heartrending desire—meet in any authentic music, whatever
the modalities of sentiment at play. For example, the first
movement of Bach's Concerto in D-Minor for two violins,
redolent with optimism, can leave an impression of melancholy, of longing for a mysterious Beyond, as profoundly as
Schumann's Piano Concerto in A-Minor, so poignantly ani-
mated by the soul's thirst for an elusive unknown. All depends

---

[5] From Baudelaire's *L'Art romantique*, cited in Maritain's *Art*, 134; 26.

on the spiritual density of the work and on the depth of silence from which it springs. This, we may add, proves yet again that the heart of music is to be found far beyond the more or less definite feelings it conveys on the surface.

It is only in works displaying true genius that these poles can merge in harmonious unity. We think of Bach, of his great edifices of sound: the Organ Works and Cantatas, or the Passions, whose wonderfully robust, fulfilling musicality seems to answer the full gamut of spiritual potential seeking freedom and perfection in man. What other music carries—by letting the two extremes so completely touch and intermingle—such certain, all-conquering faith while simultaneously opening onto an indefinite horizon? Such music is a "Yes," an "Amen" of unlimited perspectives. We hear it, gasping with desire and flooded by the joy of shadowless security. It sings of the nostalgia for death that, according to the *Little Chronicle of Magdalena Bach*, was like a wound on the great Cantor's soul.[6] But it also carries the note of gladness to which the existence of God, the grandeur of his mysteries, and the infallible accomplishment of his designs give rise in the heart of a Christian who lives by his faith. We may therefore ask whether the secret of this extraordinary genius, to whom every true musician will rally, regardless of his school or ideal, does not reside in the fact that his works respond to a twofold tendency inscribed at the heart of the human spirit: the need for the absolute, for certainty, and the need for the dream, for mystery? Bach draws them together in perfect order. Further, throughout the works of Bach we see evidence, given with calm, sure authority and communicative force, of those realities that, by the degree of their influence, are the criteria of authentic music: life, love, truth, and unity.

[6] Esther Meynell, *The Little Chronicle of Magdalena Bach* (London: Chatto & Windus, 1925), 177ff.

Music and Ultimate Values

THE REALITIES WE HAVE JUST EVOKED belong to the realm of the sacred. They flow from that sovereign music which is expressive beyond any other language. Since, as Saint Augustine says, they originate in the *penetralia* [man's "innermost sanctuary"], this is where we shall first try to examine them; later, we may trace their influence in the musical signs themselves. While not forgetting the distance that separates the world of nature from that of grace, the created from the uncreated, let us ascertain that all things issue from God's goodness. Mystery itself lies within this descending perspective, which originates in a God who diffuses and gives himself. By it, we see the degree to which music, springing from a world of unearthly silence, remains marked by the great attributes of Being, whose envoy is beauty.

Nothing is more impenetrable than life, for it is rooted in God's most hidden aspect, in him whom Pseudo-Denys calls "the fount of divinity," in the Father. In God, life and fecundity are one. For God, to live is to engender the Word and to breathe forth, with the Word-Son, the Spirit of mutual love. This threefold personhood of God is both the expression and the term of an infinite intensity of life. Because the life of God, like his goodness, is superabundant and self-giving, it pours itself out and overflows, so to speak, from the sanctuary of Divinity to create a universe of signs as a temporal prolongation of the eternal processions in which everything that exists is raised to life eternal.

It has been said that movement is life: *vita in motu*. This applies to a spontaneous, immanent movement that proceeds from the inmost depths of a being whom God quickens with breath derived from his own divine life. In God, life is at once, in the simultaneity of an eternal instant, movement and repose. It unites the impetuous, ardent, yet gentle momentum from Unity to Trinity with the immobility of a perfect peace that consummates movement in the unity and mutual indwelling of the Consubstantial Three. "Everything that movement presupposes and implies about perfection of life; everything entailed about permanent stability and perfect union by *in*-existence: all is found in the Trinity. There is no division between the two aspects, since he who is alive (the Son) is within him who is (the Father)."[1]

This is why, after the example of the life of God, our own life—our true life, welling up from an underlying realm of silence and peace far beyond superficial activity—is at once momentum and rest. In our most secret depths we are grafted onto our immovable God. From there our life, in the likeness of the life of God, springs forth in intelligence and love. The more firmly and assuredly our life rests stable on the rock of Divinity, the swifter and more energetic will be its course, enveloped by the intersecting movement of the Divine Persons.

When the artist of genius conceives a work of art, his inspiration flows from the depth of his being, where his life emanates from the life of God. His life, created as an image of his Creator, buds forth in an interior word; through the impulse of an immanent breath, it extends and eternalizes itself in his work, finding expression outside that word. The natural order knows no higher manifestation of spiritual fruitfulness than this virginal transmission of life drawn from the divine wellspring. Life generates life, as Chesterton remarked with reference to the thirteenth century's flourishing of great art, for the beauty

---

[1] J. Souben, *Théologie dogmatique: Les Personnes divines* (Paris: Beauchesne, 1903), 83.

of a work of art is essentially living and life-giving. In beauty, all the transcendentals live together in resplendent union.

We may well ask if what thus applies to every art is not especially true of music. Human genius is certainly able to harness even the dullest matter to become a conduit for the spirit. It has wonderfully conveyed life to combinations of forms, lines, and colors. *The Victory of Samothrace*, da Vinci's *Head of Christ*, or Rembrandt's *Night Watch* are works so pregnant with life that their invisible aura keeps us spellbound. But music is supremely an art of movement. At the service of creative life it places a matter so supple and fluid, so akin to spirit (and, like spirit, imponderable), that it seems tailor-made to take on all the modalities of life, from extreme force— think of some Toccata or great Organ Fugue by Bach, closing with all the authority of a gripping theophany—to extreme gentleness, as in a Gregorian melody that approaches silence by its sobriety, yet is penetrating and suggestive like the *sibilus aurae tenuis* ["murmur of a soft breeze"] which manifested God to the prophet Elijah at the mouth of the cave (1 Kgs 19:12). What work of statuary or painting, in which the most intense life freezes in immobility, carries the rolling waves of ever new, inexhaustible life that we find flowing through an oratorio or symphony? Does not the rhythm that extends in time resemble the breathing of a great living being? Do we not, in great masterpieces, see every form of movement in succession as the most varied elements intertwine, contest, and complete one another in innumerable ways without ever destroying the unity and coherence of the parts?

However, it is not only by its inhalation and exhalation, by the arsis and thesis of its rhythm, or by its capacity to render the full range of life's vicissitudes that music lets life circulate so freely. It is above all by virtue of the eternal element that is revealed to us beyond the signs of sound and by music's way of taking us there. What for us constitutes the maximum of life is eternity. In Boethius's definition, immortalized by Saint Thomas, eternity is the "entire, simultaneous, and perfect possession of life without end": *interminabilis vitae tota simul et perfecta possessio.*[2] To this eternity man aspires. He has a vague sense that his life and being are from thence suspended and that, having been projected from eternity into time, he is called to return to eternity. What is remarkable is this: that man, who in sin's wake has become a slave of time, finds his way back to eternity through time and in accordance with the laws of time rather than by some more or less illusory evasion, like that of the yogi or Platonist. Music effects precisely this passage. For while our memory records the progressive development of rhythms, of melodic and harmonic relations, synthesizing them until music's potential reaches its term and completion, we forget time. We are in communion with eternity. A friend once declared that "Nothing gives an impression of greater immobility than the performance of music with a perfectly even rhythm. A passage from the Brandenburg Concertos, once it has subjected our breathing and circulation, removes our sense of time." Is music not, in this capacity, a symbol of contemplation, which, in the immobility of a gaze fixed on God's eternal Beauty, transcends and redeems time?

♩ ♫ ♩

Even as music springs from life, it springs from love. Not from some particular love, joyful or sad, violent or calm, but from the foundational love that, beyond superficial modalities, informs all creative art of genius. Such love is grounded in the sanctuary of divine realities. We know that "God is love" (1 John 4:8, 16). Never has a more adorable word sprung from the pen of an inspired writer. I have no words to speak of the infinity of trinitarian love, its overflowing generosity, its condescension to man and all else that, in league with sin, has crucified God's beauty.

In God, love, like life, is bound up with fecundity. It is because he *is* love that God gives himself to himself with all that he is in

---

[2] Boethius, *De Consolatione philosophiae* V.6.

ecstatic contemplation of his own essence. From this contemplation proceeds the third aspect of God, the Holy Spirit. Even as
the superabundance of divine life projects God, so to speak,
beyond himself and makes him Creator, so the gift of love, which
to begin with is God's gift to God, overflows in the gift of his
Being to creatures made in his image. In them he can love himself by a reflux that prolongs the essential movement of trinitarian love *ad intra*. For there is, in the final account, a single love,
flowing from an uncreated source, that envelops and penetrates
all God has made in order to bring all things back to their eternal
beginning. If only we could enter the depths of our soul, we
should find there that singular love alive: indestructible, silent,
hidden, and ready (were it not buried and paralyzed by the
effects of our first fall) to seize us entirely and lead us back to
its source. Man scatters himself in loves that are more or less
distant derivations of, or a prelude to, or, alas, deviations from,
that one love. Human love, maintains Gustave Thibon, makes
no sense if it does not lead beyond man. We may consider him
the wisest of men who is most deeply conscious of eternal love;
him the holiest, who most fully lives out of it.

On the level of creative inspiration, the musician of genius
is in communion with eternal love. The beauty of his work
will testify to it, though he may be only vaguely aware of it.
Too often it seems at odds with his moral life, which remains
mediocre. Thibon has put forward what is probably the only
valid solution to the problematic discrepancies that may arise
between an artist's genius and his affective life: "No one can
express what he does not experience. The artist carries love
within him, but it is worked, made fruitful, and turned away
from its normal end by his faculty of expression. For that
reason it cannot blossom in itself. Its best sap serves to nurture
other flowers."[3] It is nonetheless true that love bestows itself

---

[3] *Le Pain*, 132. The author adds: "Hereby we find explained the contrast, so frequent in great men, between the splendor of a work brilliant

to all through works of art and that it finds in music a mode of expression eminently suited to itself. Love does not find spontaneous expression in words but in a language whose beauty and imprecision (the hallmark of boundlessness) seem destined to convey love's ineffable infinitude. The signs that most enchant the senses will be most apt to express love, for love delights the soul more than any other good. The multiplicity of voices and instruments that expand the potential of this language, whether they sound alone or melt together in unity of symphony, are simply a more or less grandiose amplification of the voice of a lover—*cantare amantis est* ["singing belongs to lovers"]—who would make the whole world's concert of love his own.

It is commonly said that music is made to praise, celebrate, and give thanks. But what *are* praise, celebration, and thanksgiving if not the fruits of love that has found love? The love of the pauper (himself a nothing) meets the love of him who is abundance and self-giving plenitude. Being the voice of love, music bears love's imprint in the subtle materiality of its signs. For we know for certain that love means relation, and that it is governed, in relation, by a law of attraction. Incidentally, is it not curious that the terms "concord" and "harmony," drawn from the language of music, are the ones that best spell out love's needs and triumphs in the affective domain?

While transmitting the voice of the one, eternal love, music must also respond to it. For "a great soul's love for God is as nothing compared to God's love for the soul."[4] It is our task

---

with love and the misery of a private life weighed down by meanness and selfishness. A love, a force thus 'expressed' cannot manifest and express itself normally in its proper order. It is not surprising, therefore, that beside a most pure work, great-spirited men display stunted private virtues. Their heart is like a tree that, for being devoured by a blossoming parasite, can only issue branches and sick fruit."

[4] A phrase from the *Upanishads*, that summit of India's wisdom, which surely merits adoption by Christianity.

to deliver the signs of sound of this twofold desire. Going from God to us and from us to God, it touches what is most sacred in ourselves as well as the mystery of the beyond. The precise modalities of love's passage through a heart of flesh are of little interest. But it is always the same love that is present, like a living sap binding together a host of great works from every age, nation, and school, from the Mass in B-Minor to *Boris Godunov*. Love creates the work's communicative value and impact along with its potential for communion. In the firmament of art, love's manifold resonances give rise to constellations of genius.[5]

♩ ♫ ♩

If the voice of music, for one who has ears to hear, is a call from love revealing our vocation to love, and if that voice captivates us, it is surely because, as Coventry Patmore declared, "love's the truth." Love alone makes sense of our life and being. It explains our origin, our destiny, and our final end. Sovereign music, the voice of love eternal, is also the voice of eternal truth. Beauty is the splendor of good coupled with the splendor of truth; the splendor, too, of form, as a trace or beam of creative intelligence imprinted on the heart of

---

[5] Regarding the expression of love, are there not secret affinities between, say, Mozart, Schubert, and Fauré? There are nuances, of course, for in a single trail of tenderness, intimacy, and melancholy, each has his own novel, incommunicable touch. Mozart and Schubert would seem to outdo Fauré in ingenuity. Does not the latter's caressing, more refined sweetness convey in its all-embracing charm a sensibility that is less pure and closer to the senses? In the expression of impetuous love, I am tempted to approach Beethoven and Wagner, even if the former far outweighs the latter in greatness and artistic sincerity. Yet, we should not push comparisons too far. In an area so rich and nuanced, one must take care not to categorize. Franck, for example, shows a kinship with Beethoven in his Symphony in D-Minor and his great works for piano. But has he not also, in his Pastorale or Cantabile, found a voice that echoes Mozart or Fauré?

created being. Beauty descends from the intelligible world as from a world of love. One and the same transcendent reality radiates both light and warmth.

God is truth in his absolute being, simply because he is. It follows that he is the norm of truth here below and that nothing is true except by conforming to the eternal idea that presided over its creation, the idea carried by God in his Word. Truth in God is attributed to the Word-Son, perfect image of the Father, because he represents the adequate, always active knowledge God has of himself, as the one defining measure of what is ineffable and boundless. To the Word proceeding from the Father by way of intelligence we ascribe not only truth but also beauty, the fulguration of intelligibility. Beauty is made for contemplation, even as the Word is contemplated by him who engenders it. To penetrate the mystery of the artist's contemplation, we must rise to God's own contemplation. For God, says Saint Thomas following Augustine, has made all things, under the inspiration of his Spirit of love, by his Word and by his art.

Any creation marked by genius and reflecting a ray of otherworldly light springs, before its author's reason and will unite to compose it, from the depth of the artist's being, where he encounters foundational Being. Here his soul is true, naked and virginal, unassailed by illusion. Rodin insisted that art can only spring from interior truth. The higher the source from which a work flows, the more it will conform to eternal truth and partake of the beauty of the Word. In this domain, truth is evidently not synonymous with spontaneity. The truth of a work of art will often have to be conquered. The musician who, like Beethoven, takes as his watchword "Never to betray truth!" engages in Jacob's fight with the angel, that is, with one greater than himself, against whom he must use violence. We have already touched on the labor undergone by the creative artist anxious to convey his message faithfully, a labor that goes far beyond the simple probity of a man detached from concessions to effect or success. When César Franck groped about to give definitive form to the first movement of his String Quartet, perhaps his most beautiful work, it was not simply for the satisfaction of discovering a more perfect harmonic formula but rather to render as exactly as possible the voice of inspiration that sang in his soul.[6]

In this respect, it is with truth as with love. Carried by a beauty that unites them in one splendor, both find an echo in us because it is for truth and love that we are made. A theologian might express it thus: "In creating finite mind, the absolute Infinite leaves its imprint: the opening onto infinity which renders the mind of man able to know and love infinitely. This is what signals the true destiny of man."[7] Art is the symbol, the foretaste, of that infinitude in contemplation and love which is realized by grace in the saints. Through beauty, a fullness of intelligibility is offered to our intelligence. At issue is a kind of knowledge that, as opposed to scientific knowledge, works through the senses—in other words, through the only kind of intuitive knowledge connatural to man. On such terms our intelligence at once drinks effortlessly and with delight from the brightness of Being. "The mind rejoices in the beautiful because in the beautiful it finds itself again; recognizes itself, and comes into contact with its very own light."[8] As splendor of goodness, beauty delights, awakens desire, and brings forth love. As splendor of truth, beauty enlightens. Our entire being is enchanted by beauty, for in the deep strata of beauty it recovers itself. Sovereign music, therefore, answers to a twofold demand for contemplation and love, a demand that, in us, is immense.

We can now recognize the mistake of those who see in music only a land of dreams, of elusive and illusory dreams. Its

---

[6] The various drafts can be seen in Vincent d'Indy, *César Franck* (Paris: [n. pub.], 1919), 167–69.

[7] M.-D. Rolan-Gosselin, "Démesure et mesure de l'amour," *La Vie intellectuelle* 1 (1928): 212–19.

[8] Maritain, *Art*, 20.

enthralling voice has no other purpose, they would say, than to make us briefly forget the grief and mediocrity of our existence. Music to them is like a lovely fairy tale. Let us not be afraid to affirm that, quite on the contrary, music is the land of the real. But the realities of which it sings are too pure, too high, too vast to be tied down by concepts and robbed of their secret. Music is a bridge to the divine. It is a place of encounter between him who calls us and our truest self, but that encounter is not, as we shall see, full union. It can only alert our attention to the paradisal splendor of which it is a sign and mysterious preamble, while ever broadening our desire.

♩ ♫ ♩

We have spoken of relation, life, love, and truth: values that music carries and communicates. They are aspects of a single transcendent reality that embraces them all because it is their point of departure and their end: unity. What indeed *is* relation if not an effort to attain unity and a condition for ensuring its victory? What is life, if not the movement of our being toward a perfection to be crowned by unity? What is love, if not our being's desire to realize unity in the possession of another being, or of all beings, or, supremely, of the one Being who is essential love? What is truth, if not the likeness of created being to the first unity from which it derives, the unity of the Logos, who is the exemplar of all that partakes of Being and the art of the living God? What, finally, is beauty, the beauty we have defined as unity in variety and variety in unity, if not the single foundational splendor of all the transcendentals?

God is supreme unity. If the infinite intensity of his life finds expression in a trinity of Persons, is it not, so to speak, to lead unity to its peak of perfection? Being the Unity of all that flows from his creative act, God brings all things back to unity. It has been remarked that "everything that rises will converge." Everything that transcends itself in upward movement will be drawn together and joined. This great movement toward unity transpires in music and finds in music its illustration.

Having been taught by "voices crying in the wilderness," Psichari wrote that music manifests "the momentum toward unity taken to its highest degree."[9]

The sound basis of this statement can be discerned above all by considering the values of eternity and universality of which sovereign music is an emissary. What is more one than eternity, than the eternity that appears to us in the immobility of an indivisible point, in contrast to time, which is irrefutably subject to passage and fragmentation? It is this element of the eternal that makes of music the most wonderful instrument of communion we could ever dream of, and which confers its universal character.

We have said it already: if we go to the heart of music, we see that it unites us, in the worlds of body and mind alike, to all that through the impulse of God's eternal will proceeds from God and breaks away from him, yet remains dependent on him. Man is placed as a true microcosm at the center of creation in order to seize all its harmonies. The mission of music is to be an instrument by which man is enabled not only to sense and capture the vibrations of the created universe but to express them in their subtlest resonances. These are the silent voices that, in him, take flesh and are delivered. We must cross the threshold that separates the sensible world from the intelligible world. "Sounds," said Saint Augustine, "are the light of numbers." And the law of numbers, which is sovereign in music, extends to everything. Numbers (we are still following Augustine) are the universal reality that proceeds from primal unity—the *unum principale*—and brings everything back to that unity, constituting the order, coherence, and beauty of the universe. On that basis, cannot sounds incarnate these silent harmonies in what is sensory, in order to make accessible that which impels us and beckons to us from every

---

[9] *Les Voix qui crient dans le désert* (Paris: Conard, 1920; repr. Saint-Lubin, 2008), 54.

direction, in us and around us, both in the world of divine realities and in that of familiar things?[10]

In order to enter the mystery of universal communion expressed by music, let us recall the dream of Scipio. Drawing on an idea of Pythagoras's, Cicero supposes that the suns, planets, and stars perform an immense symphony as they run their course in the firmament of heaven. Men have unfortunately lost the ability to hear it. Still, if they cultivate music and play some instrument, they realize something of the harmonies to which they have become deaf and thereby gain access to distant realms.[11] It is obvious that the story is not to be taken literally. But we may rightly consider it a valuable myth. Is this not the truth it contains: that our fallen state no longer permits us to perceive the wonderful harmony of created things, of heaven singing the power, wisdom, and beauty of its Maker? But God took pity on men. He has permitted some resonances from this prodigious symphony to reach us, to rejoice our hearts and so awaken our desire for more exalted and purely divine harmonies, and above all to help us praise him and give him thanks, since for this purpose music was made.

Music, then, is the voice of God's love for us and of our love for him; it is the voice, above all, of the prayer that flows from our innermost being. Music makes us cantors on behalf of all creation, which needs *our* soul to have a soul at all and to glorify its Creator. Job and the Psalmist perceived the heavenly concert that sings of God's greatness (Job 38; Ps 18). It must pass through us, come alive in us, to find in us its sublimity

---

[10] The Augustinian theory of numbers takes us beyond the parameters of this essay. I can only indicate those passages of Augustine's works in which the subject is treated with a profundity apt to open vast perspectives: *De musica* VI; *De ordine* II.11–19; *De libero arbitrio* II.8ff.; *De vera religione* XXXff.; *De Genesi ad litteram* I; *De civitate Dei* XII.18; *Letters* 138 and 166.

[11] The story was told in a book of Cicero's *Republic* which is now lost but of which Macrobius has preserved some fragments.

and unity. To that effect, scriptural revelation records Jubal's construction of the first string and wind instruments—the harp and pipe—in the distant patriarchal age (Gen 4:21) as an event worth remembering, for by these instruments man can express not only his interior music but also that which flows from inanimate things.

By establishing us in a relationship of solidarity with all things, music becomes almost a sacramental of unity. "God has ordered everything with number, weight, and measure," says Wisdom (Wis 11:21). Music is governed by eternal, divine laws that are inscribed on the heart of creation. It comes down to us from the sanctuary of divine realities, bearing tidings of eternal resonances and gathering the harmonies of all souls and all things so as to let the totality of many voices merge in the unity of its one voice. That is why every great composition is endowed with cosmic character, transcending time, space, and events in order to expand into the rising sphere of an assembling movement toward unity. The unspeakable happiness which music bestows—as in the *Ode to Joy* that gradually rises and intensifies into the prodigious apotheosis that closes the Ninth Symphony—is the joy of universal communion in the triumphant rediscovery of unity.

Music itself carries the mark of that unity in its basic techniques. Is it not true that rhythm, which governs melody, submits to a permanent and necessary effort of synthesis and consequently of unity? The unity of a melodic figure enters the unity of a line, which in turn enters the unity of a phrase, which melts into the unity of a section. This, at last, enters the unity of the whole piece, which stands like a chiseled, smooth rock.[12] In its turn, each movement of a suite, sonata, or sym-

---

[12] "To achieve perfect form, the work must be *one*, representing *one* direction to the mind's eye. It must constitute a whole in which individually dependent parts keep together, *cuius participatio in idipsum*, as Scripture says of the perfect city (Psalm 121). Its different aspects and successive moments are joined together by secret connections and the

phony, while keeping its autonomy, enters the greater, definitive unity of the whole work and remains dependent on it.
Here rhythm fulfills its function of simultaneous development
and synthesis. There is, then, something like a hierarchy of
several unities in the progressive conquest of an ultimate unity
whose sublimity and grandeur correspond to the rich com-
plexity of the elements it assimilates.

The aspiration to unity also finds expression in procedures
that belong to the architecture of music but remain nonetheless
the fruit of inspiration: in a melodic theme that imposes itself,
sometimes obsessively, as the element from which everything
begins, on which everything converges, and by which everything develops; in a leitmotif that forms the backdrop against
which everything else in an opera or oratorio comes to life, a
few bars that distill the essence of the drama and bestow its
particular aura, investing each detail with a mysterious, implacable resonance; or in the persistent bass so wonderfully
used by Bach and some of his precursors to provide, notwithstanding occasional rhythmic dislocation, an unassailable
stability capable of sustaining ingenious, sometimes exuberant
fantasy without losing anything of its authority or call to unity.
Think of Bach's great Chorale on the *Credo* or of his incomparable Passacaglia; or of the Passacaglia and two Chaconnes
by Buxtehude, the master organist whom Bach admired above
all others.

Let us finally observe that music also tends toward unity by
the manner in which it takes hold of us as listeners. Penetrating
through senses charged, so to speak, with intelligence, it seizes
us entirely, making our interior and exterior senses one. In this
respect music creates in us a (fugitive) state analogous to the
supernatural contemplation that draws the soul beyond itself

---

internal logic that assure the vital unity of a living organism." Henri
Davenson, *Traité de la musique selon l'esprit de Saint Augustin* (Neuchâtel:
La Baconnière, 1942), 169.

with such sweetness and force that all man's faculties, sometimes even his body, are torn from themselves in order to be drawn together, and at the same time lost, in God. It restores man to the beauty of his primordial oneness with all things. At one with his uncreated source, how can he fail to be one with himself, his fellow human beings, and the entire cosmos? Indeed, he can no longer return to himself, for he is part of the beloved. *Ekstasis,* the departure from self through love's force of attraction, is a phenomenon of which, humanly speaking, the musician has some experience. For as long as he is subject to the seductive power of music, he too is transported to a mysterious Beyond and is once again one: everything he is, everything he has, is absorbed by his mind, in touch with the eternal world that is his true homeland. The tidings he receives from this country overwhelm him, rather as God, by his grace, overwhelms the deified soul freed from sin and re-conformed to its Creator. Music is truly the heart of the eternal God, who speaks to those who seek him in time. One who hears this voice and transcends himself at its call recovers unity through the touch of that Beauty which, as we have seen, is the one, unifying splendor of all Being's attributes.

Ernest Psichari was right to maintain that music is the rightful homeland of mystics who crave the life of union.[13] Saints, as long as they remain on the way toward innocence regained, are given over to the unifying power of love. In them, the ferment of unity that secretly works the entire human race through rifts and strife reaches its furthest potential. Like the martyr Ignatius, saints are "set on unity,"[14] thirsting on their own behalf and on behalf of all men for the unity whose supreme expression at the end of time will be, in Saint Augustine's gripping phrase, "One single Christ loving himself,"[15]

[13] *Les Voix*, 54.
[14] *Phil* VIII.
[15] *In Epist. Iohann.* X.3.

or, as Saint Paul puts it, "God being everything in everyone" (1 Cor 15:28). In such men and women, everything is attuned, everything sings in obedience to God's rhythm and eternal designs. Let us hear one such soul who, under God's touch, produced some of the loveliest spiritual music the world has ever heard. I mean Catherine, the sweet virgin of Siena. God told her what souls are like once good order is established within them:

> The soul's movements, then, make a jubilant sound, its chords tempered and harmonized with prudence and light, all of them melting into one sound, the glorification and praise of my name. Into this same sound where the great chords of the soul's powers are harmonized, the small chords of the body's senses and organs are blended. . . . They are pleasing to me, pleasing to the angels, pleasing to those who are truly joyful, who wait with great joy and gladness for the day they will share each other's happiness, and pleasing to the world.[16]

Did not even Saint Thomas speak of a spiritual melody, an intelligible song arising from thoughts and affections that are conducted by God according to proper rhythm and order?[17]

Every order, every beauty, and every unity, like all relation, all life, all truth, and all love, are eminently present in him who is himself Musician and very Music: Christ Jesus. In the absoluteness of his twofold nature and person, he incarnates all the values that have come down to earth from God and rise back

---

[16] Catherine of Siena, *The Dialogue*, trans. Suzanne Noffke, Classics of Western Spirituality (London: SPCK, 1980), 310.

[17] *Sicut ergo in locutionibus exterioribus secundum melodiam et proportionem prolatis resultat cantus sensibilis; ita in locutionibus interioribus et etiam affectionibus secundum proportionem et ordinem debitum ad Deum directis resultat quaedam melodia spiritualis, et quidam cantus intelligibilis.* [This passage, long attributed to Thomas Aquinas, in fact comes from the Prooemium of Aegidius of Rome's *Commentary on the Song of Songs*.]

to their source through him. He alone can say: "I am truth, I am life" (John 14:6). He is "the one who loves us" (Apoc 1:5). His Person is altogether reference to his Begetter—relation to the Father. He is the most beautiful of the children of men and the splendor of the Father's glory (Ps 44; Heb 1:3). In him shines order: that is, the numbers or universal rhythm by which all things return to their origin in consummate perfection of unity, with their hierarchy and end harmonized by a unique and eternal design. At the end of his life on earth, between the Last Supper and the cross, his last words prayed imploringly for a unity so perfect that it must have as foundation and exemplar the unity of the Divine Three which will also be its fulfillment. "Father, may they be one as we are one, may they be perfected in unity" (John 17:23). Christ is, in Ruusbroec's words, the sole Conductor of a universal symphony that embraces even the groaning of material creation as it waits in pangs of childbearing for the full redemption of the sons of God (Rom 8:19-21).

It is above all to those who cling to him in unity of spirit, who are his fullness, his body, and in whom he pursues and accomplishes the work of redemption, that Christ extends the intoxicating harmony that he, more than anyone else, has let us hear. "The first," Saint Catherine of Siena goes on,

> to sound forth the sound of life was the gentle and loving Word when he took on your humanity. On the cross he made a sweet sound with this humanity united with the Godhead, and he caught all the children of the human race [on this instrumental hook]. He also caught the devil, for he took away from him the lordship he had had for so long because of his sin. All the rest of you sound forth when you learn from this maestro. The apostles learned from him and sowed his word throughout the world. The martyrs and confessors, the doctors and virgins, all caught souls with their sound.[18]

---

[18] *Dialogue*, 310f.

He whom the first Christian converts from paganism liked to call "the true Orpheus," whose voice even wild beasts obey, directs and gives life to an immense symphony that embraces the totality of time and space, "resounding from east to west."[19] He reconciles in himself the most violent contrasts, re-tuning a world troubled by the dissonance of sin. He came down from the center of divine unity in order to enter into man, who is the center of creation, carrying in his person all the harmonies of God, those of the visible and invisible worlds, of creation and redemption. He came to bring all things back to their head (Eph 1:10), to seize all things and bring them back to the Father's unity. On that unity rests a great, victorious consonance that is the concord in unity of the Consubstantial Three. The Father himself lives, loves, and sings in those whom Bossuet, without oratorical hyperbole, qualified as "hearts sighing for union."

For such as these, as for Ernest Psichari, sovereign music is not so much the memory of paradise lost as a foretaste of paradisal happiness in the City-Spouse told of by the Seer of Patmos. In that city, unity is queen. In it, there is but one light (that of God and the Lamb), one life (flowing from the throne of Majesty), one love (of God loving himself in and through his elect, filling them with joy), and one relation (resting on the perfect consonance of God and those who are his, with angels and men forming a single society).

In that city of relation restored fully and forever, there will be no more tears, says the Apocalypse (21:4) with an accent of admirable tenderness. The reference, I think, is not only to the tears of sorrow whose dignity is to be, if we follow Saint Augustine, "the heart's blood,"[20] but also to the complex tears that are called forth by the shock of Beauty and that signal, as

---

[19] *Chorus Christi ab oriente in occidentem consonat* (Augustine, *Enarr. in Ps.* CXLIX).

[20] *Sermon* LXXVIIB. 6.

we have seen, both happiness and nostalgic desire. We shall then be so perfectly adapted to the perfect harmony of God and of all that makes up the invisible world, so profoundly immersed in the security of our Homeland and the inalienable joy of our vision, that the infinite beauty of what we see, of what we taste with our minds and glorified bodies, will attain a region in us that is free from all sensory feeling. Everything that the purest and most intoxicating music of this earth carried by way of promise and virtuality will blossom forth in praise, and that praise will have no end since our love will be endless. *Sine fine erit laus, quia sine fine amor* ["praise will be without end because love will be without end"].[21]

---

[21] Augustine, *Enarr. in Ps.* CXLI.19.

Music's Mission

BY DISCOVERING IN SOVEREIGN MUSIC the imprint of values both human and divine that respond to our deepest desire, we have ascended to that intelligible, silent, transcendent music of which every work of genius gives some presentiment when it leads us beyond itself (and ourselves) to the sphere of mystery and eternal realities whence it flows. We cannot, however, accomplish this passage without the aid of grace. Music is an incarnation of God's beauty and of the universal harmony of things and beings in the magic, seductive world of sound. In a hierophanic universe, music is a sign. Like all signs, it carries the risk of attaching us to itself instead of delivering its spiritual content. Because it is a sign, music is a message. As such, it betrays itself—no, we betray *it*—when, enthralled by its beauty, we remain incapable of going beyond it in order to attain the naked reality signified. The sign of the beautiful is not the beautiful itself, however much it may be bathed in its glory. It is the eternal beauty behind the sign we must attain, even as we have to perceive the voice of a super-human, heavenly call through the voice of sound.

Because it is a sign and a message, music is also, in this world where all is grace,[1] a gift—a gift more precious than

[1] "The world tirelessly nurtures my existence. The air does not hold back from my lungs, the seasons welcome me as their guest, while an army of chance occurrences fights my cause. A miracle of protection, of maternity and clemency, suffuses with light every step I take. A hand that never contracts in refusal dispenses my soul without respite, and

any other for those who are able to understand it, love it, and grasp it in its pure essence. Unfortunately, it is precisely when music reaches its loftiest peaks, when, overflowing with life and love, it captivates us with its peculiar impact of prodigious enchantment, that it risks becoming a danger. This shows us the degree to which we are wounded by sin.

Indeed, there is a problem, or rather a drama of art, which we cannot pass over in silence, for it allows us to sense art's mystery. Over against a theory that would reduce art to mere technique or entertainment, strangely underrating the extent to which its momentum transcends the natural plane, stands a conception that tends to see art as a supreme good, as an absolute. "Art engenders false gods," said Léon Bloy, and such idolatry is perhaps more disastrous than any other. Money, sex, science, or progress are likewise false gods that dry up the living sap of one who gives himself to them with that hunger for the absolute that God alone can quench and fulfill. But because the delights of art are spiritual, because they respond to our noblest tendencies, it is sometimes more difficult to transcend them in pursuit of the true Absolute which they symbolize or prefigure than in the case of those other, crumbling idols that disintegrate and unmask their lie as soon as man, by turning within, takes note of his dignity and greatness. The religion of art is not merely a mirage; it is a profanation with regard to God, who alone deserves our adoration. If he has been pleased to let his beauty be incarnate in lines, forms, words, or sounds, it is only so that these may attract us to himself. Even the most sublime music will never be more

---

likewise the length of days, which I in turn squander" (Thibon, *Le Pain*, 16). From a more exalted point of view, the statement "all is grace" belongs to souls who consider the ways of God with shattering lucidity. It expresses the attitude before death of St. Thérèse of Lisieux or of a hero from the fiction of Bernanos. In this sense music too is grace, for it opens onto the sacred. Its mission is to lead us to God and to awaken our nostalgia for death.

than a means, a call, and a bridge to the kingdom of the absolute.

Let us be more specific. In a vigorous article, Stanislas Fumet has uncovered and refuted the idolatry of art by showing that the aspirations of the human mind made manifest by art, however stirring, are only the shadow—the exact, magic shadow—of the aspirations we discover in the abyss of our soul. Our soul is conscious of this fact as long as it is willing to learn from the voices of silence. Art is divine, but it is not God, and Fumet does not shrink from ascertaining definitively that we are not made for the divine but for God alone. His assertion corresponds to a profound truth and is not at all paradoxical. That which issues from God as divine keeps us back in the *idea* of perfection. It can veil from us the personal God whose radiance it is, who through signs calls us to himself.[2] This is so true that in order to touch God in the joy of contemplation we must first allow ourselves to be torn away from the divine. We must be stripped by grace in the midst of a purifying night that is the mystic's profoundest pain. Aesthetic beauty, on the other hand, seizes us without any preliminaries of asceticism, as if we were not sinners at all, but already fit for its glorious happiness. We should not, therefore, be afraid to underline the distance that separates divine grace from its symbol or preamble.

We have seen that art is an unknown world of joy and grandeur that exceeds us yet is also familiar inasmuch as it accords with our deepest self. The reality of this world of mystery, however, does not readily surrender itself to us. The most authentic music may fill us with a sense of deliverance and lead us beyond our own limits and the limits of all creation; it nonetheless eludes our grasp. Even if it leaves behind indefinite resonances in our soul, it escapes us and leaves us in

---

[2] Stanislas Fumet, "La Tentation du divin," *La Vie intellectuelle* 2 (1929): 942–53.

suspense. It is very true that we need in some way to be distanced from the beauty which engages our contemplation. It has even been said that "distance is the soul of the beautiful."[3]

At the same time we know that our moral being is in no way altered by this mysterious contact with the divine, which infuses us with its lifeblood and opens us up but cannot transform us. Only grace can work our transformation and grant us, if we are faithful to its promptings, to obtain God by re-creating us in his image. If we refer to the insight procured by poetry or music as "mystical," we do so purely by analogy, because it is an intuitive insight void of concepts, like that of mystical contemplation properly so called. It has likewise been said that poetry, and music too, "is supernatural in a relative fashion. It does not stand above the order of created, creatable nature, for this is the prerogative of the absolutely supernatural, but it stands above sensory nature and the assembled laws of the material universe, and its values belong to the transcendental order."[4]

Notwithstanding the harmony that binds together the order of nature and that of grace; notwithstanding the mysterious attraction that makes the former tend toward the latter while the latter crowns and perfects the former: there is in reality a chasm between the two that can only be bridged by the extravagant love of a personal God and by Christ's redemptive incarnation. Likewise we have identified, between the inspired artist and the saint, the distance that separates God's inspiration *qua* Creator from God's inspiration *qua* Redeemer and Sanctifier. The creative musician may be called divine (Germans speak of "the divine Schumann"), but after the fashion of the hero, not of the saint. Already the philosophers and theologians of antiquity recognized that musicians obey an inspiration of a special kind, belonging to the natural order

[3] Simone Weil, *Gravity and Grace*, 136.
[4] Jacques Maritain, *Réponse à Jean Cocteau* (Paris: Stock, 1926), 23.

but situated above deliberative reason. Saints, meanwhile, are moved by love flowing from the Holy Spirit, who is the burning heart of the Blessed Trinity, issuing from the eternal embrace of the Father and Son.

The artist carries an Edenic message capable of bestowing on men an exalted spiritual joy, while the message of the saint plays a very different role, being situated beyond death, outside the grasp of sin. The one brings to men a life-giving work resplendent with the brightness of Being. The other is himself God's masterpiece: the living product of the inner life of its Author, who tirelessly perfects it.[5] The artist separates himself from his work by creating—and we know, alas, the rift that may obtain between a work infused with love and beauty, and the moral deficiencies of its author. The saint is one with his work, for his work is his person, his life. Everything in him is love and seized by love. Capturing the harmonies of the universe, the former completes the work of creation by which things flow forth from God and are detached from him, though not without keeping some trace of him. The latter is placed at the center of unity from which all harmony springs and on which it converges. Thus he completes the work of Christ's passion (think of Saint Paul's mysterious *desunt* ["what is lacking"] in Col 1:24) and participates in the return of all things to God in the immense movement of "recapitula-

---

[5] Saint Irenaeus expresses it splendidly: "O man, you who are the handiwork of God, await the artist's touch. He will work everything in the best possible way. Offer him a heart that is supple and docile. Maintain the imprint that the artist has given you. Do not lose your plasticity, lest you forfeit by hardening the marks left by his fingers. If you keep the relief, you will rise to perfection, for God's art will adorn what is but clay. His hands have fashioned your substance. He now comes to clothe you with pure gold and silver within, while without you will be so splendidly embellished that the king will himself desire your beauty. . . . If only you give him what is your own—that is, your trust and your obedience—his art will fashion you and you will be God's work of perfection." (*Adv. Haer.* IV.39.)

tion" wrought by Christ the Mediator. The artist lives immersed in creation and sees himself coexisting with all beings in immense solidarity. The saint contemplates creation illuminated by the gift of Wisdom and thus transcends it while yet remaining profoundly one with it, for he loves it with God's own charity. Saint Francis's salutation of "my Sister Water, my Brother Fire" is not merely a poetic formula full of charm. It expresses a rare and personal experience.[6]

Artist and saint are both listeners. One listens in order to capture the secret, silent voices of nature and things. The other listens in order to perceive in the depth of his soul the voice of God, who has established his dwelling within it. It is at once the voice of a father, brother, spouse, and friend, of a being who in the unity of his nature is adorably personal. Both artist and saint are at the same time at one with the universe and separated from all. For the former, these contrary poles create a rift that contributes poignantly to the pain that is inseparable from genius. The latter finds the contradiction resolved in love. The saint's poverty of spirit ("*Blessed* are the poor in spirit") may lead him into the deepest desert, but this desert will always, in naked faith and far from all created things, be inhabited by God's fullness, by all that is alive in the invisible world, and by that which, in the visible world, passes through his soul in order to find his way back to God and praise him. Like God himself, he is solitary, but never alone.

I have said that music is given us to celebrate and give thanks. The saint exposed to the Spirit's touch is himself the perfect instrument for voicing the "praise of glory" in answer to an ineffable design of eternal love. By virtue of his free communion with him who is infinite life, he is a being essentially alive. And "the man fully alive is God's glory."[7]

---

[6] Cf. G. K. Chesterton, *St. Francis of Assisi* (London: Hodder and Stoughton [n.d.]), 101ff.

[7] Irenaeus, *Adv. Haer*. IV.20.

Music and the Sacred

IF I HAVE DRAWN ATTENTION TO THE GULF that separates a saint from a genius, it is certainly not with a view to denigrating the value of aesthetic beauty. By virtue of this beauty, which descends from the transcendental realm in order to become incarnate here below, art is enabled to "present an intrinsic affinity with religion," as Pius XII declared.[1] Although art should never become the object of a cult, it is nonetheless religious in its highest spheres (whether it is Greek, Egyptian, or Chinese) and should normally lead us toward him who is the sole object of religion: God. Simone Weil is right to note that God is really present in everything that awakens in us an authentic sense of beauty. She adds that the world contains a kind of incarnation of God which has beauty as its hallmark.[2]

Still, we are well aware that the divine presence we encounter in beauty may leave us strangers to God and to his call. "You were with me, but I was not with you." Such was Saint Augustine's admission to the God he had sought too exclusively through creatures and not sufficiently for what God is in himself. Sadly, his cry too often corresponds to reality. Our blindness before the splendors of creation is a more or less distant echo of that which marked the pagans berated by Saint Paul (Rom 1:18-23).

Even the artist who produces works resplendent with light and joy (thus prolonging the creative act whereby God makes

[1] Allocution of 8 April 1952.
[2] *Gravity and Grace*, 137.

80

all things by his Word) may have only the vaguest idea of God. He may declare himself an atheist. He does not know God, even if he perceives in things a mysterious Beyond that delights and torments him. The poet, for example, may know nothing of that which makes up the living realities of the supernatural world

> nor of the bonds which in actual existence attach poetry and beauty necessarily to God; or if he does, he knows it only in so confused a way that he can either reject, in so far as his own human choices are concerned, the *élan* which traverses his experience, or divert its trend and stop at the mirror by turning aside from the too real Immensity which it enigmatically reflects. Thus, many poets are convinced that all poetry is religious by essence, though they hardly believe in God or confuse him with nature.[3]

In order to attain God deliberately and effectively through a work of art, it is quite certain that we need grace, not in the broad sense of the word, as when we say that "all is gift" or "all is grace," but grace in the theological sense, as an enlightening, dynamic help reaching from the heart of God to our own soul, aiding us to be more divinely human and to find our fulfillment beyond ourselves, in God. This is what really matters: to attain God *through* God as he speaks within us, as he speaks through the things that surround us, and, most particularly, as he speaks by the radiance of his beauty. We must be penetrated by God and raised up by him in order to find God beyond everything that is commissioned to tell of him.

If we pause for a moment to consider the apparent paradoxes of art and its effect on us, we shall be better equipped to understand the exalted and unique role of music as well as the end

---

[3] Jacques Maritain, *Approaches to God*, trans. Peter O'Reilly (London: Allen & Unwin, 1955), 72f.

to which music leads us. We have already observed that we find joy in the act of perceiving beauty. This joy is able to refine mere sensual joy, which it far exceeds, by educating the latter to be stirred only by spiritual things. It likewise surpasses the joys felt by the speculative intellect in its slow and laborious quest for truth. Yet while beauty brings us joy, it also tears us apart. Authentic art does not simply satiate. The more it is pregnant with divine values and the purer the joy it procures, the more intense and painful is the rift it causes.

Aside from this indefinable impression composed of fullness and regret, of appeasement and disquiet, we find that we are captivated by music only insofar as we are set free, by music's charm and despite ourselves, from the created order and from ourselves. Music takes hold of us, in Nietzsche's phrase, by "liberating forces that cause us to suffer by their very abundance." In the same way, the eternal frees us from time, infinity from what is finite. But what is this unknown before which beauty places us? Is it accessible and knowable? If its mystery is so far beyond man, why is it bestowed on us? Why does it fill us with happiness while, at the same time, it eludes our grasp? Why is beauty at once so distant and so near? What lies concealed in its bosom?

According to Bergson, the sole object of beauty is to eliminate what masks reality from us and so to place us face-to-face with reality itself. An encounter face-to-face is not an embrace; indeed, it renders an embrace impossible. Distance, therefore, is the soul of beauty. Saint Thomas defines the beautiful as *id quod visum placet* ["what pleases when seen"].[4] It is made not to be embraced but rather to be seen and heard. Yet this beauty, which effortlessly fixes and subjugates our attention, is but a symbol. It evokes another, supernatural contemplation that is the fruit of grace, and this grace is itself a deifying, unifying reality, alone capable of working this wonder: it keeps us,

---

[4] *Summa Theologiae* 1a.V.4.

however high we may rise, at an ever infinite distance from him who is essential Beauty, while uniting us with him to the point where we are penetrated (as Saint Bernard expressed it) like iron in a forge, like a drop of water poured into a cup of wine, like air bathed in sunlight. Only in the encounter with God beyond signs will our joint desire for contemplation and union, like a moth's yearning for the stars, find fulfillment by the work of grace. Music draws us toward that of which it is the call and premonition but which it cannot bestow. To obey the call of music, we need grace. Such grace may be accidental, but it tends, always and essentially, toward permanence. Like a spark sprung from God's hearth, it is ready to enkindle the same flame in our innermost being.

Grace alone can intimate that for us, poor sinners who cling to sensible realities, sovereign Beauty is a thing too pure and too great, even when it descends in the signs that express it, for us to make it our own and to enter its mystery, which is not of earth but of heaven. Grace alone can make us understand that the attractive force of art requires us to transcend ourselves and all things in a liberation from the tyranny of egoism, to whose dominion we are all unconsciously subject.

But now to a most serious and weighty question: From where can such grace come? From God, obviously, but not from a vague and abstract God: from a God, rather, who is personal and who was crucified; from a God who became man so that men might become God. There can be no grace except through the cross of Christ, the cross that commands a sinful yet redeemed world, winning it over to the Father. All being, all life, every destiny hangs upon it. It is the kingly, salvific, and divinizing cross of a God who, before rising again, carried his *kenosis*—his annihilation—through to the end, and who leads us after himself, in order to raise us up in him and with him.

Christ and us: one reality. His drama is ours and ours his, continuing through time and space until his second coming. The great Pasch of the Lord, which, from Calvary to the empty tomb, saw life springing from death, is our Pasch also. The

great crossing *(Pascha)* which took place once and for all and
of which the Jews' exodus was a figure and promise is also the
continuous crossing accomplished throughout our individual
existences, even as it takes place for all humanity throughout
history. We are the prolongation and fulfillment of Christ here
below. The Christian drama is this: to pass with him, in him,
through the great waters of death—a daily death that is consummated only when our body dies—in order to live by his
unfailing life. For he has returned victorious, his humanity
suffused with glory in trinitarian splendor. This drama is hidden, but essential. Compared to it, all other dramas, however
poignant and serious, are mere eddies on the surface of the
pool in which sinful humanity rises toward redemption.

At stake in this terribly serious drama is our eternal destiny,
beyond earth, to be gods by participation. It is the drama of
our faith, and faith is nothing other than the plunge into an
unknown that surpasses us, of which sovereign music brings
a kind of revelation and foretaste. Sadly, too many men and
women are fearful of the unknown and proclaim, like the
self-declared sage in Paul Claudel's lovely *Diary of Christopher
Columbus*: "We are of the opinion that the unknown is always
something unpleasant." And why? Because the unknown
brings risk, and because risk jostles us in our comfortable
cowardice, calling us to be generous and strong. The risk in-
creases in proportion to the magnitude of the outcome at
stake. But do we not all carry in us what we need to overcome
any risks brought by our nature and vocation?

Insofar as its value lies in what it suggests rather than in
what it realizes, art does not immerse us, despite ourselves,
in the depths of the ocean of the divine. It invites us, rather,
on a journey. It invites us to look for our unique and universal
homeland, the enchanted country dreamt of by the poet
Baudelaire:

> *Where order and beauty is all,*
> *Comfort, peace and pleasure.*

This is not a vain dream of an earthly paradise shut forever but a lawful dream that corresponds to the paradise God has revealed in a splendid vision through the last prophet of the new covenant. We all yearn for this paradise, albeit unknowingly, for, as Claudel exclaims:

> *All men are called to yonder shore.*
> *Please God to let us reach it.*

Like our forefather Abraham, we must depart toward that which we have never seen but only heard God speak of, and God, as the catechism of my childhood put it, "deceives neither himself nor us." We must be on our way, strong in the promise that resounds from age to age with ever more magnificent assurances and a note of ever closer intimacy. We must leave all, pressed by a hope that has the measure of the faith and charity on which it rests and to which, in turn, it gives wings. Our departure must be such that the thought of turning back is ruled out. So intensely must we desire this unknown, this great and holy risk that entails the acceptance of death and the loss of all creatures (a promise so wonderful could require nothing less) that everything seems simple, that we choose and love everything that occurs to us on our crossing to love's absolute.

"Go, Child of God! I am with you. Go! Go!" These words were heard by Joan of Arc. If we take refuge in the silence of our own depths, we can all hear the same voice driving us, like the Maid of Orleans or Columbus, toward the unknown of our destiny and the accomplishment of our particular mission, a mission which is most often hidden in the secret of God's countenance but which will one day shine forth in splendor, when we stand forth as who we really are.

Is not the interiorizing, uplifting force of music singularly suited to lead us into the heart of the desert where Moses met "Him Who Is"? God invites us all there to celebrate with tenderness, in faith (Hos 2:19), the eternal marriage feast which the whole Bible announces and prepares, and which sovereign music makes us discern and desire by marrying, through beauty, the ephemeral and the eternal. For like all art, music maintains an eschatological character alongside its aspiration to re-create heaven and earth and to fill us with paradisal happiness. It tends toward a paradise that is already truly begun in the luminous, sorrowful shadowland of faith—toward a heavenly paradise of vision and glory. In and through creation, music pulls us away from ourselves and all created things. It invites us to shed everything that keeps us from obtaining our purpose. By the reality it signifies, music belongs on high; by its signs of sound, it belongs here below. Thus it espouses the paradox of man, who is body and mind, a pure image of God yet drawn out of nothing, pulled as if on a cross between, on the one hand, this present world of fleshly, transient, and visible realities and, on the other, the world of the changeless and eternal. According to Saint Paul, the imprint of our baptism has made us a new creation. Music enchants by telling of a world renewed. It is the only stage worthy to produce the marriage of the Word and redeemed humanity, the feast whose symbolic, profusely splendid representation is the last seal placed on the revelation of Jesus by his prophet (Apoc 19–22).

We can only grasp the eschatological character of music in the light of the reality that lies hidden beneath the sign and by virtue of an interior disposition for which music can only prepare us. If there is an affinity between religion and art, may we not be permitted to think that music at its best presents some harmony with the liberating, life-giving breath of the Spirit of truth and love, to whom Scripture attributes "the voice's skill" (Wis 1:7)? Theologians, it is true, ascribe beauty to the Word.[5] But given that music is the most immaterial,

---

[5] "The elements of Beauty are most clearly manifest in the second of the divine Persons, who is the radiant image of the Father's perfection, the expression and manifestation of all that lies hidden in the Father.

penetrating, and intoxicating expression of this beauty, may we not legitimately place it within the realm of the Spirit, the dispenser of divine gifts, the motive force of fruitful vitality, the great worker of unity? In the sphere of grace, the Spirit stirs and develops the infused virtues of faith, hope, and charity. Without the Spirit's refreshing breath, they would remain three magnificent yet cold and dead planets in our soul's heaven. The highest Christian truths would run the risk of remaining for us mere objects of speculation, a distant and abstract reality, did not the Spirit who is *lumen cordium* (the light, that is, of all our love and desire) bestow on them both savor and attraction and the power to transform our entire being, to guide it with gentle force to its destiny.

Who could measure the impact of resonances born through the shock of this beauty in a soul that through grace has become God's dwelling place? We find ourselves, here, at the summit of the natural order, in the pure atmosphere of transcendentals radiant with beauty. Is it not music's prerogative, by virtue of its universality and by the rustle of eternity it carries, to make supernatural truths penetrate more deeply by disposing us to receive them? Does it not operate in the manner of a spiritual energy fit to acclimatize souls to invisible realities? Does it not render realities charged with divine love sensory, so to speak? Over and beyond its status as a symbol of the Spirit, does not authentic music possess the power to stir the soul's secret potential and thus to facilitate the Spirit's work in us? Could it not become in some way a coadjutor of the Spirit, fulfilling the function of adapting us to God through the divine element already inscribed in art? We shall have occasion to come back to this question when we look at sacred chant, which in this respect, as in its inspiration and purpose,

---

Therefore the Fathers and theologians attribute God's beauty chiefly to the second Person of the blessed Trinity" (M. J. Scheeben, *Dogmatique*, trans. P. Belet, 4 vols. (Paris: Palmé, 1877), 2:224).

surpasses all other music. Let us be content for the present to indicate the influence of music on a few holy souls that loved it like a cherished homeland.

We think for example of Philip Neri, the friend of Palestrina. One of his best biographers, Cardinal Capecelatro, has maintained that to leave the love of music out of the Life of Saint Philip would be to reduce the man by half and to rob his holiness of one of its most salient, most lovable traits.[6] We think of Newman, who toward the end of his life of hardship and labor picked up again the violin he had fervently cultivated in his youth. On returning to the Beethoven Quartets he had once played with poor Blanco White, his emotion was great. We can only cite the end of a letter he wrote at that time, so moving in its simplicity:

> I had a good bout at Beethoven's Quartets . . . and thought them more exquisite than ever—so that I was obliged to lay down the instrument and literally cry out with delight. . . . I really think [the fiddle] will add to my power of working, and the length of my life. I never wrote more than when I played the fiddle. I always sleep better after music. There must be some electric current passing from the strings through the fingers into the brain and down the spinal marrow. Perhaps thought is music.[7]

Or we think of Yvonne Bisiaux,[8] the young artist whom music did not retain but dispatch, rather, beyond herself toward God

---

[6] Alfonso Cardinal Capecelatro, *The Life of Saint Philip Neri, Apostle of Rome*, trans. Thomas Alder Pope (London: Burns, Oates & Washbourne, 1926), 384.

[7] Cited in Wilfrid Ward, *The Life of John Henry Cardinal Newman Based on His Private Journals and Correspondence*, 2 vols. (London: Longmans, Green, and Co., 1912), 2:76.

[8] Yvonne Bisiaux (1893–1919), endowed with rare musical talent at a very young age, entered the Carmel of Pontoise in 1914 and took the religious name Marie-Angélique de Jésus. —Ed.

in the solitude and silence of Carmel, where she died prematurely in the odor of sanctity. "I have never been able to understand," she said, "how one can make music and not become a saint; how one can love music without desiring to be one." We may object that this is to confuse categories, to ignore the line that separates the natural from the supernatural, the aesthetic from the mystical. The distinctions are useful, even necessary. But let us go deeper and follow the logic of a recovered innocence that, beyond sin and death, penetrates to the reality of the sign and identifies this reality as the sacred. The important point is this: that the beautiful and the sacred are inseparable. One is the radiance of the other, and both together offer themselves to us as a reality so powerful, so dense that it cannot but be transformative, like the *res* transcending and fulfilling the sacrament. In the brightness of the sign that, although it abides (for naked realities are not for this world), yields up its content, there is nothing profane left. There is only the sacred.

This alliance of holiness and beauty appears above all in the angelic sphere, in the invisible world where myriad pure spirits move as perfectly limpid reflections of the Deity. And ultimately God himself, who in the unity of his perfections alone is Holy, is infinite Beauty. Once we have identified the danger of art that betrays its mission by holding us back in created things (what Berdyaev called an "art of satisfaction"), once we have established the distinction between aesthetics and morals that is called for here below, we need not hesitate to claim that beauty finds its normal perfection in the sacred. Rainer Maria Rilke, with his profound intuition of the angelic world, sensed this deeply. If the presence of one of these pure spirits were to become sensorily manifest, it would, he proclaims, crush him through its spiritual density:

> *Supposing that one*
> *would suddenly seize me*
> *and press me to his heart.*

I should perish by force of his overpowering presence.
What is terrible arises out of beauty.[9]

That which appears beyond creation as terrible—*tremendum*—is God in his absolute transcendence. He is the One, the entirely Other, the thrice Holy before whom powers tremble, whose sight cannot be sustained even by the Seraphim while they endlessly chant their triple *Sanctus* as an echo of the praise God renders himself in the mystery of his trinitarian life. He is the God whose presence Jacob felt twice with terror and whom he called "the Dread of Isaac" (Gen 31:53). Even in the majestic gentleness of his incarnation, God caused Peter to withdraw with fright, exclaiming, "Depart from me Lord, for I am a sinful man!" (Luke 5:8). Who is pure before the Holy One? Who can endure the closeness of him who is fullness of Being? Who can bear the touch or sight of his blinding light and burning incandescence?

And yet the *Rex tremendae maiestatis* ["King of terrible majesty"] is also *fascinans*. He is the reality that irresistibly captivates and draws us by his very excellence, by the radiance issuing from his sovereign majesty as well as by the kindness of his love. Oh the weight of God's love! It could crush us to death, but instead draws us toward him by acting in our heart of hearts, where by infinite condescension God chooses to dwell, quite without forfeiting his infinite transcendence. His love resembles fire, which rises in pursuit of its own gravity: *Pondus meum amor meus* ["my weight is my love"].[10] The finality of music, then, and the finality of all authentic art is the sacred, the wellspring of the sacred: the God who is Beauty.

---

[9] Rainer Maria Rilke, *Duino Elegies*, I.

[10] Augustine, *Confessions* XIII.9. The passage continues: "Wherever I am carried, it is he who bears me. Your gift sets us ablaze and raises us on high. We burn and rise. We cross the threshold of our soul and sing the song of ascents. Your fire, your beneficent fire, consumes us as we proceed, as we ascend towards the peace of Jerusalem."

This union of beauty and holiness has been probed by the Church, and the Church has given it its highest illustration by letting art, and music in particular, enter her liturgy.

Music and Liturgy

THE SACRED LITURGY FLOWS FROM THE HEART OF THE CHURCH, that great contemplative. As Spouse of Christ and Mother of all the faithful for whom Christ died, she knows what is pleasing to her Master, what gives most fitting honor to the Blessed Trinity, and what best contributes to the good of her children. Ordained to dispense the grace flowing from Christ to all her members, continually irradiated by the Spirit of truth and love, the Church's highest function here below is to sing with Christ the New Song foretold by the Prophets. "In taking on human nature, the divine Word brought into our exile the hymn which is chanted eternally in heaven. He unites the entire human race to himself, and in union with it sings this hymn of praise to God."[1]

Through this hymn of adoration, which Saint Hildegard of Bingen saw implanted in the Church, like Christ's body in the virginal womb of Mary, by the Holy Spirit,[2] the Church is ultimately tending toward the glory of the Father, toward that which, so to speak, is most impenetrable, most silent in the Godhead: the Father, inexhaustible source of life and tender love to whom, after making him known, the Son and the Spirit are commissioned to bring us back.

In her function of worship, the Church can offer to God only what she has received from him, for of ourselves we possess

[1] From Pius XII's encyclical *Mediator Dei*, 144.
[2] *Letter* XXIII to the Prelates of Mainz.

nothing. At the heart of the Mystery of Faith, the Church performs her offertory, with thanksgiving, *de donis ac datis* ["from the gifts given"], giving back to God his own good gifts, transformed by his redemptive, sanctifying power in infinite mercy. In the same way, the priest (and with him, the whole Church) at the heart of the liturgy takes bread and wine, the humble elements which sustain our earthly existence, and transubstantiates them into the holiest and most beautiful substance that heaven and earth have ever brought forth, the Body and Blood of God: the bread of the strong and the wine that makes virgins fruitful, which will one day unite the whole company of the redeemed into a single risen body in the Risen One.

It is from these same *donis ac datis* that the Church finds means to establish, around the Mystery of Faith, her sacrifice of praise, "the fruit of lips that confess God's name" (cf. Heb 13:15). In this instance, however, she does not choose from among lowly substances sprung from the soil, but looks instead to the very highest of gifts, to that which is most spiritual both in the order of grace and in the order of nature. She looks, that is, to the sacred text which for two thousand years has constituted God's revelation to mankind, inspired words which the Spirit spoke through the mouths of prophets and which, as an incarnation of the Word, are destined to be eaten and drunk as a kind of eucharist.[3]

Henceforth, the Spirit, who prays in us with sighs too deep for words (Rom 8:26f.), works an encounter with himself in the Word of the Scriptures and of the liturgy, for in the Church's worship it is ultimately God who reaches out to God through us, in order to lead us toward the abyss of the Father.

---

[3] "Drink the draught of the Word from both the Old and the New Testament, for in both you drink Christ. . . . We drink, we ingest the Scriptures when the juice of the eternal Word descends into the veins of our mind, into the essence of our soul" (Ambrose of Milan, *In Psalmum I Enarratio*, XXXIII).

And this is the point at which art, especially music, enters the picture. If, *de donis ac datis*, the Logos hidden in the sign of written words is, in the supernatural order, the highest gift given to men and that most worthy of praising God thrice holy, then music, by its kinship with the Spirit, by its power to penetrate the most hidden regions of the soul, is surely, in the natural order which it tends by inspired movement to transcend, the sign most apt to adorn the Word? And not only to adorn it, but to collaborate with it and constitute, as it were, a commentary upon it. "I wish my people to pray with beauty," declared Saint Pius X, while he was working for the restoration of Gregorian chant.[4]

What was needed was a form of art which transcends art, music which transcends music; an *inspired* music, not in the technical sense in which God's Word is inspired, but gushing forth from the Spirit of sevenfold gift, the Spirit, above all, of Wisdom. The Spirit has "probed the depths"[5] of contemplative souls in order to bring to birth melodies worthy of the sacred Word, which invest that Word with transfiguring

---

[4] Before going on to speak about Gregorian chant, we think it necessary to warn the reader that it is extremely rare to find this music executed with the perfection required for listeners to appreciate the extent of its beauty. This fact is due, it would seem, primarily to factors of the spiritual order. From a technical point of view, the plainchant melody rests on a certain number of very simple principles, but these must be perfectly assimilated if they are to be practiced with the mastery, flow, and suppleness required by such exquisite art. However, the Gregorian cantilena further presupposes a mentality imbued with the supernatural—a spirituality intimately attuned to the mysteries of the liturgy, made up of humility, serene enthusiasm, and a spirit of worship. This is something one does not often encounter, even among the most devout Christians.

[5] In the text *Instituta Patrum*, which introduces the Solesmes *Graduale* of 1908, we read: *Haec de gremio sanctorum Patrum collegimus; quorum quidam hunc modum cantandi ab Angelis didicerunt, alii, Spiritu Sancto rimante in cordibus eorum, per contemplationem perceperunt* (XIV). The force of the verb *rimor* (to "excavate," "search closely into," "explore") is difficult to render.

power by awakening, far beyond man's intellectual bound-
aries, the unsuspected depths of his being; for it is a music
capable of introducing us to the heart of Mystery simultaneously through our purest affectivity and our most spiritual
sensibility.

These souls were those of the monks of old who, during a
golden age of a few centuries before and after Gregory the
Great, succeeded in translating the Church's contemplative
soul into her function of worship. Such is the value and range
of these sacred melodies that great liturgists and musicians
who have examined them closely—for their wonderfully expressive beauty as much as for their technical aspect—have
boldly declared that, if we wish to possess the prayer of the
Church in its fullness, we must seek it not only in the breviary
and missal, but also in the gradual and antiphonary.

Naturally, we must not be exclusive: Gregorian chant is not
the only kind of music to possess a sacred character. We have
already seen that all great art is, by its nature, religious, and
among the masterpieces which have as their object the one
true God, which have besought, praised, and adored him, we
cannot neglect the musical value—the accent of purity, fervor,
and heavenly peace—inherent in the admirable polyphonies
of Palestrina, Lassus, and Vittoria, for example, not to speak
of more recent works, from the Mass in B-Minor to the Re-
quiem of Fauré or Duruflé. It goes without saying that these
works are the fruit of superior technical insight and more developed art, of an art which is consciously art, placing at the
disposal of beauty resources that in earlier times were un-
thought of. And yet, let us not be afraid to say as much: for
every receptive, bare, and silent soul responsive to the realm
of mystery, the Gregorian melody will never lose its primacy.
It is imbued with a special grace by the nature of its inspiration
and spiritual quality. With minimal sound material, it produces
maximal expression. Free from all human admixture, divine
grace at its humblest and at the same time most glorious forms
an alliance with that in the realm of matter which is most subtle

and akin to the spirit. The resulting sign is utterly transparent
to that which it signifies—a reality inexhaustible in its divine
depth—and art ensues, as it were, by gratuitous overflowing,
as the simple effulgence of the sacred. For these reasons, Gregorian chant constitutes a unique phenomenon within the
domain of music, one which can only, such is our conviction,
be revealed to souls already attuned to the supernatural.

By turns spirited and subdued to the point of a whisper,
always lyrical (of a lyricism sometimes dense and close to
silence, sometimes expansive, but rarely exuberant, for it possesses a sacred modesty and an instinct of a higher order),
always abounding in life, Gregorian chant is, we might well
say, the quintessence of music. Enthroned as a queen in beauty,
it originates where all music should lead. It brings us in touch
with eternal truths, not, as in the case of other music, even of
genius, through the intermediacy of a human personality,
temperament, race, nation, or any other interplay of multiple
influences, but directly. In it, the current that transmits is
adapted to the source whence it springs. It knows what is to
be known about God's transcendence and creative love, about
our fall, and about the redemptive love which restores us to
our origin. In the manner of Wisdom, it "pervades and penetrates all things because of its purity" (cf. Wis 7:24).

Like the Spirit of love shining about the Logos that breathes
it, the chant is arrayed with beauty, *splendor veri, splendor boni,
splendor formae* ["the splendor of the true, the splendor of the
good, the splendor of form"]: the inspired Word which, in
turn, inspires it. It is placed at the service of that Word to
unveil its secrets and release its fragrance. Even as the Spirit
is commissioned to introduce us to the mysteries of the Logos,
so the chant incarnates the Word within us by its interiorizing,
illuminating operation. For the Word is a two-edged sword,
revealing the hidden places of the heart and piercing the depth
of souls in order to carry out its work of division and judgment
(cf. Heb 4:12), while the chant that envelops it, to which it is
wedded with such a wealth of ineffable nuance, is like a spiri-

tual ointment. With infinite tenderness, it permeates and suffuses, poured out like the "waters of Shiloh which flow gently" (Isa 8:6)—an apt symbol of God's grace, which transforms without indiscretion or violence.[6]

Through all this, we can see that, if there is an art which betrays its message by subjecting us to created things and to itself (which is precisely the nature of sin), and if there is, by contrast, a redeeming art which detaches us from creatures in order to lead us to the reality it designates, then the Gregorian cantilena is an art so deeply imbued with the supernatural that it is impossible for souls to submit to a superficial seduction cut off from the chant's sublime content. No one can really understand it without first being conformed to its mystery through love.[7]

We have seen that all music, as a fruit of human genius, addresses that center of the soul which, in solidarity with all creation, opens onto the Essence in which all things are grounded by the roots of their being. The sacred chant likewise reaches out to the innermost depths of our soul. But it touches the soul not merely as being in process of creation; it touches it as redeemed and in process of re-creation by a life-giving death toward which, as we know, all authentic art ultimately points. And so the whole universe, groaning for its freeing and the full revelation of the sons of God, sings through us and in us, who are its soul and mouthpiece as well as its crown, in a new solidarity going infinitely beyond that which had but our common creation for its origin. *Omnis terra adoret te et psallat tibi* ["May all the earth adore you and sing to you"] (Ps 65:4), proclaims a Gregorian introit almost ecstatic in its immaterial beauty.

---

[6] Cf. J. Guillet, *Thèmes bibliques* (Paris: Desclée, 1951), 254–55.

[7] Simone Weil is no doubt right in saying that "a person who is passionately fond of music may quite well be a perverted person—but I should find it hard to believe this of any one who thirsted for Gregorian chant" (*Gravity and Grace*, 138).

If it is true that the value of art inheres in what it suggests rather than in what it accomplishes, then this principle is particularly applicable to the Gregorian melody, which remains always on the threshold of silence. It emerges from an ineffable mystery only to immerse us in it. However, what it does accomplish, in a different sense, is the transformation of souls that surrender themselves to its sacred influence. For the contemplative whose daily bread it is, the chant, while having worship as its first object, is equally a powerful aid to the interior life and to inner purification. As we have seen, it presupposes that we have in some measure been conformed to the mystery; it then plunges us further into the depths of the divine by stripping us of everything earthly, by transfiguring us in the image of the Word which it continually extols, the Word which is Christ. Thus, there can be no better definition of this music, which sanctifies because it is itself sacred, than the formula used by Pius XI to describe an eminent degree of holiness: "possessing peace in its fervor, and fervor in its peace."[8]

In the realm of the sacred, the New Song succeeds better than any other music in uniting love's ardor to order's calm; it indicates more clearly than any other music could the eschatological character of art. And how could it be otherwise, given that it has already tasted the firstfruits of the Spirit, whose constant prayer is, "Come, Lord Jesus!"? Thus it translates the immense longing of the Church militant to reach at last the dwellings of eternity.

Naturally, the chant is also, like other music, infused with nostalgic yearning and with joy. But through its medium, these two sentiments, apparently opposed, cause no disquiet in the soul that lives and probes them with the clear insight of faith. On the contrary, such a soul perceives the harmony of their coexistence. For by means of songs so full of humble

---

[8] Discourse on the decree *De tuto*, on the canonization of Blessed Pompilio Pirrotti.

supplication and glorious trust, the Church communicates the secret which she alone possesses: her sense of what man is— man, who is so pitiable in his earthly condition, yet so sublime in his vocation as a child of God, already betrothed to and incorporated into Christ by the Spirit, and already returning to the Father through Christ and through the Spirit.

The vibrancy of these melodies is a burning desire, the fruit of a "hope which does not deceive" (Rom 5:5) and of a yearning for ineffable realities only dimly perceived here below. They give voice to the love of *viatores* ["wayfarers"] "on pilgrimage far from the Lord" (cf. 2 Cor 5:6) yet pilgrimaging *toward* the Lord. They resemble the songs of ascent that accompanied the Jewish people going up to the earthly Jerusalem. A song of yearning, yes, but also and above all a song of joy, of joy too deep to be expressed by fanfares. For it already echoes the eternal rejoicing of the marriage feast held in the splendid City of espousal (cf. Apoc 21). When an earthly dwelling resounds with choirs and music, says Augustine, we know that a feast is being kept in honor of a birth or a wedding:

> But in the house of God, the feast is everlasting, since that which it celebrates is not ephemeral. The angelic choir amounts to an everlasting feast; the vision of God is perfect joy. This day is a feast without beginning or end. From that spiritual feast, a mysteriously sweet and musical echo resounds in the soul, if it is not drowned by the world's clamor. In one advancing towards the wonderful tabernacle of God and considering God's wonders in the redemption of his faithful, the ear is tickled with delight at the sound of the feast, while the deer is drawn to the wellspring.[9]

♩ ♫ ♩

There is only one liturgy, one single concert of praise, in heaven and on earth. With the angels, "who unite themselves

---

[9] Augustine, *Enarr. in Ps.* XLI. 9.

to us on account of Jesus, our common Master, though ours more than theirs,"[10] we form a single choir which embraces in its union the entire visible cosmos of inanimate creatures. It is a great honor for the Christian congregation to be invited, at the most solemn moment of the *mysterium fidei* ["mystery of faith"], to effect a *sursum corda* ["lifting up of hearts"], to participate in the spontaneous worship of pure spirits and to sing with them the threefold Holy of eternal adoration.

For angels do sing.[11] But how? We are powerless to imagine it, given that their song is of the order of pure intelligence and could only, it would seem, become sensory through an inter-

---

[10] Bossuet, *IVe Lettre à une demoiselle de Metz sur l'unité de l'Église*, cited in Peterson, *Das Buch von den Engeln: Stellung und Bedeutung der heiligen Engel im Kultus* (Munich: Kösel, 1955), 7. This is a traditional view, dear to Saint Augustine. See also the last chapter of Mère Cécile Bruyère's *La Vie spirituelle et l'oraison d'après la sainte Écriture et la tradition monastique* (Tours: [no pub.], 1920; repr. Sablé-sur-Sarthe: Solesmes, 1984).

[11] Newman speaks of it poetically in the *Dream of Gerontius*: "The sound is like the rushing of the wind—the summer wind among the lofty pines; swelling and dying, echoing round about, now there, now distant, wild and beautiful; while, scattered from the branches it has stirred, descend ecstatic odours. . . . But hark! A grand mysterious harmony: it floods me, like the deep and solemn sound of many waters." The tradition of the Fathers maintains that the angels sing with a single voice. Their chant, in other words, is monodic, not polyphonic. From this, Erik Peterson deduces that monastic chant should likewise be monodic, for it is the song of "men whose entire existence is lifted out of the natural order of things, who have drawn near to angelic being." For the same reason, Peterson adds, the early Christians rejected any intrusion of musical instruments into the Church. After the Ascension, "the Apostles left behind the earthly Jerusalem and its Temple music and approached the heavenly Jerusalem where no instruments of any kind are found, since the angel by his very existence is a unique organ of divine praise. It is not, then, surprising that the musical instruments mentioned in the Psalms were interpreted in relation to the existence of Christians. 'You are the trumpet, psaltery, zither, drum, chorus, organ, and sweet-sounding cymbal. You are all these things. There is in this nothing unworthy, transitory, or theatrical.' These are Augustine's words in his exposition

vention by the angels themselves, in a gesture of condescension to our carnal condition. Even so their song would be perceived only by the most interior senses of the soul, refined by the grace of divine union, as in that "concert of silence," that "resounding solitude" which Saint John of the Cross speaks of in his *Spiritual Canticle*. If we are to believe Walter Hilton, the grace of hearing this song is sometimes granted to souls who have arrived at perfect charity, to console them in their earthly exile:

> This song cannot be described by any bodily likeness, for it is spiritual, and above all imagination and reason. It may be felt and perceived in a soul, but it may not be showed. Nevertheless, I will speak of it to you as I think. When a soul is purified by the love of God, illumined by wisdom, and stabilised by the might of God, then the eye of the soul is opened to see spiritual things, as virtues and angels and holy souls, and heavenly things. Then, because it is clean, the soul is able to feel the touching, the speaking of good angels. This touching and speaking is spiritual and not bodily. For when the soul is lifted and ravished out of sensuality, and out of mind of any earthly things, then in great fervour of love and light (if our Lord deigns) the soul may hear and feel heavenly sound, made by the presence of angels in loving God.[12]

This seems to have been the case of one of Hilton's contemporaries, the holy hermit Richard Rolle, who gently, patiently, and through many trials, entered, as he says himself, "into the freedom of the light." If we turn to the account he left of his mystical experience, we learn that it came to him one day in the form of a *canor*, a "chant," that thenceforth never left him. He was busy singing the Psalms when:

---

of the 150th Psalm, but they no less express the conviction of all the Church Fathers" (*Das Buch*, 43f.).

[12] From Hilton's brief treatise *The Song of Angels*.

> I beheld above me the noise as it were of readers, or rather singers. Whiles also I took heed praying to heaven with my whole desire, suddenly, I wot not in what manner, I felt in me the noise of song, and received the most liking heavenly melody which dwelt with me in my mind. For my thought was forsooth changed to continual song of mirth, and I had as it were praises in my meditation, and in my prayers and psalm-saying I uttered the same sound, and henceforth, for plenteousness of inward sweetness, I burst into singing what before I said, but forsooth privily, because alone before my Maker.[13]

Was this not a foretaste, in angelic communion, of the music of paradise, granted to a soul almost entirely purified? Probably. What is certain is that, in the case of Rolle, the experience of this *canor* was joined to the painful call of a yearning to see God, which nostalgia for death served only to intensify.

Without pretending to be favored with comparable gifts, the ordinary monk devoted to praise and contemplation knows full well that the merely formal union of his worship to that of the angels, following the solemn invitation extended to all Christians, is not sufficient. Living as he does at the heart of the Church, his Mother, the praise of God is his special function, his *raison d'être*, and so it is with entire spontaneity that he unites his worship, his adoration, his song to that of the angels, his brethren. Without wanting to become an angel himself, he understands that he must become as like one as possible, to share not only in the angels' song but in everything that constitutes their life and calling. As Erik Peterson puts it:

> Man is but one part of creation, necessarily established in relation to other beings, among whom are the angels and

---

[13] *The Fire of Love or Melody of Love and the Mending of Life or Rule of Living Translated by Richard Misyn*, bk. 1, chap. 15, ed. Frances M. M. Comper, with an introduction by Evelyn Underhill (London: Methuen, 1914), 70.

demons. It is important to remember that angelic beings are not just something in relation to which our human nature was established at its origin; no, it is in this relation that it continues, here and now and for ever, to be established.[14]

Self-transcendence is the natural condition of man, who, as man, can only realize himself by going beyond himself. That is why the truly spiritual person rejects everything from here below and, in the words of the Psalmist, "ordains an ascent in his heart" (Ps 83:6, Vulgate). He strives to move upward, ever further upward, until he reaches God, his goal. The proper sphere of this self-transcendence is that of the myriad angels who worship the Lord, in whose company, under the direction of Christ, the sole Precentor, mortals too may praise the "Father of infinite majesty" (*Te Deum*).

In becoming holy so as better to worship God, and in finding in this worship the strength we need to advance in virtue, we shall rise ever further until we reach the point at which, like the angels, we ourselves become entirely a hymn of praise. And that is the highest degree of music man can know.

The liturgy, in its annual cycle of feasts centered on the paschal mystery, transports the attentive and recollected soul into this ascent, into the divinization of beings that seek to be nothing but a pure resonance of God. In a suggestive image used by Dom Odo Casel, the liturgy acts like a spiral of which every identical circle begins one level up from the one preceding it, until it reaches its end in eternity. The liturgy shapes us even in the depths of our unconscious. Through it, the soul establishes and hides itself, little by little, in that "freedom of the light" which Richard Rolle speaks of. There, with face unveiled, reflecting the Lord's glory as in a mirror, man is transformed from glory into glory in the image of Christ, by Christ (cf. 2 Cor 3:18).

[14] Peterson, *Das Buch*, 62f.

It follows that men and women devoted to liturgical prayer must constantly rise higher, ever higher, until they become true companions to those firstborn children of God who live in beauty without a shadow of darkness, ceaselessly chanting, not with their voice, but with their very being, the *Trisagion*. Naturally, this self-transcendence is not reducible to the moral order (although it entails constant growth in moral perfection). It is metaphysical. Its goal is to bring man to praise God, in song and silence, by a cry welling up from the innermost core of his being, giving voice to his being. Having thus been made a "praise of glory," he will, in the harmony of his soul, himself become pure music. He will gain access to the mystery of music, though without ever fathoming it. For music opens onto the sacred and is, as it were, fixed in the region of the sacred, in which everything lives and breathes through the presence of him who is Holiness, Beauty, Love, drawn toward him in reverent fear and all-satiating joy. As man approaches the source of music, not as a distant, indefinable *abstractum* but as Someone—as Someone who is All—he realizes that, even here on earth, all is music and all tends toward the music of eternity. Enlightened by the foremost of signs, by the cross placed at the summit and heart of the world, he sees all other signs, including that of music, gradually fading and almost vanishing, like a veil becoming increasingly transparent and ready to reveal, fully exposed, the reality it covers.

Having transcended music and all other things, in the sphere and by means of music, man will perceive the history of this world in whose battle he is still engaged as an immense symphony resolving one dissonance by another until the intonation of the perfect major chord of the final cadence at the end of time. Every being, every thing contributes to the unity of that sublime concert, that intelligible composition, which can only be heard from within: sin, death, sorrow, repentance, innocence, prayer, the most discreet and the most exalted joys of faith, hope, and love; an infinity of themes, human and divine, meet, flee, and are intertwined before finally melting into one according to a master plan which is nothing other than the will of the Father, pursuing through all things the infallible realizations of its designs. "O wondrous poem of transitory things!" exclaimed Saint Augustine. In that poem, every verse, every note has its proper place, and through it all things and beings make their return journey, by a variety of courses, to the immense ocean of Being.

Man will further understand that everything he used to love in beautiful music was part of a search, not for something, but for Someone; that every work of genius aspires to prayer and is only the temporary resting place of an absolute value. On this level of insight, any apparent conflict between art and morality is resolved, for beauty and goodness are one, revealing their complete identity when beauty, at the furthest boundary of the sign, appears in naked splendor. Man will know by experience that the indefinable emotion procured by music is but an anticipation of its end in the all-fulfilling joy of the City of God. For Jalal al-Din Rumi was not mistaken when, in ecstasy, he called the voice of the violin "the sound of heaven's gates opening."

Finally, man will discover himself in that which is primary and intrinsic to his vocation as a creature:

> How remarkable that man, in the ontological order of his metaphysical roots, expresses the created, lowly nature of his being by beginning to rise higher, by joining company with the cherubim and seraphim, and yet, even when he is one with them, can say only this: that he is nought and stands before God purely as a hymn of praise![15]

This work is wrought by Christ himself, the great harmonizer of the visible and invisible cosmos. And it is surely no

---

[15] Peterson, *Das Buch*, 65.

coincidence that the saint who more wonderfully than anyone else realized that he was, with the rest of creation so fraternally disposed towards him, but a resonance of God, should himself receive the seal of conformity to Christ by the imprint of the stigmata after seeing the vision of a crucified seraph.

For we must speak of the Poverello of Assisi, God's troubadour, whose chanting soul was carried by music to the gates of Paradise. There is probably no better way of closing this chapter than by invoking his memory. True, our only evidence comes from the *Fioretti*, which are avowedly a legend—but a legend which may serve as a solid foundation, for it communicates more about the spirit of Saint Francis than any materially faithful but lifeless history.

Consumed by austerities, consumed above all by love, Francis was reduced to a fluttering breath. Yet he was carried away by such joy that he needed to sing, deceiving his waiting and yearning for death. His soul was so flooded with music that, to release the overflow, he imagined he could express in vibrant melody the song welling up from the depths within. He seized two small pieces of wood that lay by the wayside and used one as a fiddle, the other as a bow. He was already transported by something of heaven's glory, of which he had received a foretaste a few months earlier in the solitude of Monte Alverna. That experience had been granted him in the way which was best attuned to his soul, that is, by music, or rather, by a single sound of such beauty that it alone contained more music than all earth's symphonies. But let us rather hear the voice of the devout narrator:

> When Saint Francis was much weakened in body, as much by his great abstinence as by his battles with the devil, he desired to see his body comforted by the spiritual faculty of his soul, and so began to think of the immeasurable glory and joy of the saints in heaven, asking God to grant him by grace some foretaste of this joy. As he was dwelling on this thought, a marvelously splendid angel appeared to him of a sudden, holding a viol in his left hand and a bow in his

right. Francis stood amazed at the appearance of the angel, who a single time raised his bow upon the viol. And forthwith such great sweetness of sound invaded Francis' soul, releasing it from all bodily sensation, that, as he later told his two companions, had the angel brought the bow back upon the viol, his soul would, for an excess of sweetness, have left the body.[16]

What could we possibly add to this account? Saint Francis has brought us to the threshold of the music of eternity!

---

[16] From the end of the *Second Consideration on the Stigmata*.

The Music of Eternity

"THE EYE OF MAN HAS NOT SEEN, nor has his ear heard, nor has his heart conceived the things God has prepared for those who love him" (1 Cor 2:9). The beatitude in store for the elect is certainly a mystery, and the splendors of the Church triumphant glimpsed by the Seer of Patmos are only symbols fit to indicate something ineffable. Yet we know for sure that man's end will be to give glory to God (Eph 1:12-14). Thus, the grand liturgies that punctuate the Apocalypse correspond to an eternal reality, when the praise of the elect will mark the accomplishment of God's eternal plan of love, realized in his beloved Son. This act of praise will spring forth from within the great and endless Sabbath as the sole, prodigious activity of the blessed, who will neither tire of it nor be sated with it. It will represent the full flowering of their entire being which by now is immersed in the divine, for "God will be all in all." Further, it will be the supreme manifestation of the life our Lord came to earth to give in abundance (John 10:10). *Gloria Dei vivens homo* ["the glory of God is man fully alive"].

At the end of the *City of God*, Saint Augustine sets out to give us some idea of the beatitude of the elect. He searches for words and seems to stammer, finding human language quite inadequate to translate that which exceeds all thought. At last he shows us, in an outline of admirable progression, the vision attained at the heart of repose, the love that flows from the vision, and the praise that is the fruit of this vision and love. Its sound is without end, even as the vision and the love are endless: *Ibi vacabimus et videbimus, videbimus et amabimus,*

amabimus et laudabimus. Ecce quod erit in fine, sine fine ["There, we shall be fully at leisure and we shall see, we shall see and we shall love, we shall love and we shall praise. This is what will be in the end, without end"] (XXII.30).

What will this praise consist in? We may suppose that melodies and harmonies hitherto unimaginable for their intoxicating beauty will resound at the heart of the City-Spouse, amid the symbolic sparkle of gold, crystal, and precious stones bathed in the singular light of God and of the Lamb. We may expect music attuned to the holiness of these wonders as we evoke the Jerusalem above, our Mother, in the joy of her accomplished childbearing and of her victory, *Plena modulis in laude et canore iubilo* ["full of melodies, in praise and joyful song"] (Lauds hymn for the Dedication of a Church). This heavenly music will surely be endowed with infinite potential for responding fully to the liturgical exhortation: "Dare to praise him as much as you can, for he is beyond all praise and you can never celebrate him enough" (*Lauda Sion*).

Let us go through the Book of the Apocalypse and attempt to understand more fully how this homage of praise will be paid, gathering details of the heavenly liturgy, which, on the other side of the veil, is closely united to the liturgy on earth, as if to show us how far eternity is already present in time, and how time is suspended in eternity.

First of all, we see the angels: those who preside over the unfolding of time and those who are appointed to oversee the forces of nature, being thus established in closer solidarity with the world and the Church. Accompanying themselves on zithers, they sing the new song of mankind redeemed, while thousands of other angels add to their praise by echoing their voices. Everything culminates in an "Amen." Then the angels who surround the throne of God prostrate themselves in silent adoration (5:8-14). Further on, in a liturgical setting no less grand, we hear the "new song" of those who are pure, the one hundred and forty-four thousand whose voice resembles great waters and peals of thunder accompanied by harps (14:2-4). Then the conquerors of evil appear, likewise equipped with zithers and harps, upon a sea that is clear as crystal and glowing like fire. They sing the canticle of the old and the new law, the canticle of Moses and that of the Lamb, to proclaim the exalted works of the Almighty, the justice of his ways, and the victorious holiness and goodness of the eternal King (15:2-5). At last, the eternal Alleluia sounds like the combined voice of an immense crowd, resembling great waters and roaring thunder, in the joy of God's victory. The members of the choir are beside themselves with joy, for a radiant vista opens before them: the marriage of the Lamb, the Word of God, to his Church. They already contemplate the Bride robed in purity and glory through the virtue of her saints. Their praise becomes ecstatic, and they are reduced to crying, "Amen! Alleluia!" On that note of an immense, prodigious symphony, time terminates just as the royal and divine horseman appears with his army to overthrow Satan. Everything leads us to believe that this symphony will never end. In heaven and on earth, now transfigured and renewed, all voices will blend in harmony to form a chorus of cosmic grandeur and solemnity, surpassing any music that has ever been performed on this our humble planet lost in stellar space (19:4-7).

But, one might say: since God is ineffable, since for souls graced with the gift of contemplation he is even here below "the Beauty that shuts our lips," is not silence the only praise worthy of him? *Tibi silentium laus* ["for you, silence is praise"], we read in Psalm 65:1, following the Hebrew text. The objection deserves to be taken seriously. It can, it seems to me, be answered in two ways.

First we may remark that, while in heaven we shall live more closely united to the angels than here on earth, we shall not be pure spirits like those firstborn sons of God.[1] The body

---

[1] "All creatures, visible and invisible, have a bearing on the Church. The angels are the ministers of its salvation, and by the Church new recruits

of each of the elect will be united to the glory of his soul, and one who has been created a man by an irrevocable, infinitely wise design of God's goodness will always remain a man even if he comes, as the Lord affirms, to be *like* an angel. Man will not be fully himself until he recovers his glorified body after the Second Coming. Saint Bernard put it well: "The soul makes progress when it sheds the body. It reaches perfection when it takes it up again."[2] Just as our soul, suffused with God, will somehow be diaphanous and reveal God, so, by one and the same outpouring of light, our spiritualized flesh will be diaphanous and reveal our soul, becoming the soul's perfectly responsive instrument. Our members and our senses will praise God. Freed from every constraint, from every earthly necessity, their sole exercise will be praise.[3] We are touching on a mystery, for in order to know how adoring souls perform their praise in a manner at once sensory and immaterial, immersed in the divine, we would need to know the properties of their glorified bodies, their suppleness, subtlety, and freedom, and of these properties no earthly body can give an adequate idea.

A second argument rests on the belief that realities that cannot occur simultaneously on earth may well do so in heaven, the homeland of unity. Here below, music and silence occur in succession so as to redeem each other's poverty. But will it be likewise in heaven? Why should the two not coexist where all is unity, completion, and perfection? In our present state of wayfarers, we sense that silence is something very great. In the words of Louis Lavelle, it is "homage rendered to the gravity of life." For ascetics, it bears a purifying power

---

are made for their legions, left despoiled when Satan and his accomplices deserted" (Bossuet, *IVe Lettre à une demoiselle de Metz*).

[2] *De diligendo Deo* XI.

[3] Cf. Saint Augustine, *De Civitate* XXII.30: "*Omnia membra et viscera incorruptibilis corporis, quae nunc videmus per usus necessitatis varios distributa, quoniam tunc non erit ipsa necessitas, sed plena certa, secura, sempiterna felicitas, proficient laudibus Dei.*"

for which there is no substitute; for contemplatives and saints, it is the normal atmosphere of divine intimacy and the fruit of intense, ecstatic wonder. "Let the engendering of God be honored in silence," exclaimed Saint Gregory Nazianzen. According to Saint John of the Cross, it is "in silence that the soul hears the Father silently bringing forth the Son."

At first sight, silence appears to be characterized by the absence of sound and thus to be something negative. Yet on a higher level we sense that there is a positive silence, a silence which indicates not absence but presence, not emptiness but fullness. This silence is a language of incomparable nobility. It arises when man has relinquished all being and yet, far from being obliterated, finds himself bathed in a sea of reality, beyond the world of appearances, in the presence of "Him Who Is." This language too has its rhythms, melodies, and harmonies, though only our interior senses can perceive them.

Perhaps I may draw on a memory to evoke this silence for those who have experienced it. It is the impression of rapture that seizes us when we reach the summit of a mountain after a long ascent and find an all-enveloping solitude in which nothing, not a breath of wind, not a vibration, intrudes to trouble the utter calming of life. We do not suffer this silence. We hear it; or rather, we listen to it with the most silent part of ourselves. All the world's voices combined could not match its sweet and profound majesty charged with life. It is the fruit of superhuman peace. It is like a transparent veil before the most exalted presence. Within this silence, the course of time seems suspended. The world of earthly realities has not disappeared, but we have left it behind. From this we may get an inkling of the silence that will envelop and penetrate the city built on a hilltop when the living God, the God who is an abyss of silence and who manifests himself to himself in silence, will at last be all in all.

Yet it is precisely at the heart of this abyss that silence and music seem spontaneously to join their most secret prerogatives in order to bring about the fullness of creation's worship

of God. One expresses the ineffable nature of him who surpasses all praise; the other, the endless exaltation of love. One
conveys a state of fullness in possession, of unchanging, perfect peace; the other, of an ever new wonder before God's
beauty in the inexhaustible happiness of a limitless desire, a
desire ever quenched, yet ever craving more. Seen thus, music
no more undermines silence than the purest, most human
mysteries of our Lord's or our Lady's life undermine the ineffable trinitarian depths in which they are immersed. For contemplative souls (like that of Ignatius of Antioch[4]), the
mysteries of salvation constitute a voice resounding within
that eternal, inviolable silence in which the Consubstantial
Three see and love one another. It is exactly the same with the
praise of the saints in heaven. In a prodigious symphony of
majesty, force, and diversity, it will, in communion with the
purely intelligible adoration of the angelic spirits, echo the
praise of the triple *Sanctus* that accompanies the unfolding of
divine life and extends its open-ended enclosure of silence
round the abyss of Divinity. This symphony is a supreme
manifestation of the beauty of God communicated to creatures
by the Word, in the Spirit. It no more disturbs the silence of
the eternal aeons than the Trinity springing forth from Unity
alters that Unity. Here, music will be the perfect unfolding of
silence, which, by it, comes to recognize its own depth.

♪ ♫ ♪

We may equally suppose that, as a further prerogative, the
music of the elect will constitute their only language. The
word will so fully be a part of song as to be indistinguishable
from it. In support of this hypothesis, we may note with Kressmann that music at the beginning, when man was still in a
state of innocence, must have been inseparable from speech.[5]

---

[4] *Letter to the Ephesians* XIX.
[5] E. Kressmann, *De la musique religieuse* (Paris: Je Sers, 1944).

At that point, speech was not the dry, graceless succession of words that, when amplified, rises to become the confused roar of a crowd. It was, rather, a harmonious flow of sounds whose beauty gave voice to the charm and joy that governed man's relations with God and with his neighbor. Sin has vilified and profaned the speech that marked the nobility of man, enabled by his intelligence to utter a word in the image of God. From being at one with music, the word tore away and became autonomous when it answered the enemy's invitation and so became an instrument of disobedience. Here as elsewhere, the effect of sin is rupture. From this point onward, the word would be isolated in a world of escalating perversity. It would be the vehicle of error among men, and also the instrument of God's chastisement:

> With the confusion of tongues that followed the building of the tower of Babel, a long series of divisions began for the human race, divisions of race, nation, and language that will continue to cause war, conflict, and misunderstanding until the reign of God is finally re-established.[6]

We are well aware, however, that God's tactic for manifesting his glory is to vanquish enemies with their own arsenal: the tree with wood (as the Passiontide Preface puts it); Goliath with his own sword. In the same way, the word has become for us a great means of redemption and salvation. Through the voice of the law and prophets, the word revealed God to his people; it taught that people and ceaselessly directed it toward the coming of a Messiah who would be the Father's eternal Word incarnate. *Verbum caro factum est* ["the Word became flesh"]. God himself came as Word to converse with mankind. By virtue of words more penetrating than a two-edged sword, Christ, the Word-Son, has re-created man in his own image, reconciling all things with the Father. After return-

---

[6] Anselme Stolz, *L'ascèse chrétienne* (Chevetogne: Amay, 1948), 165f.

ing to the Father, Christ sent the Apostles his Spirit of love to
enable them to baptize and convert the world by the word.
By then, flaming tongues had symbolically manifested a creative effusion of unity that counteracts the confusion of Babel.

For the time being, however, human speech is still at the
disposal of error and sin. Only at the end of the world will it
be fully redeemed, wonderfully transfigured, and lovelier still
than it was in the first Eden. I like to think that speech will
then become music and melt into the symphony of universal
praise like an immense and endless "Alleluia" voicing all
worship, all adoration.[7] By virtue of its nobility, it will endure
forever, contributing its own note of affirmation and precision
to the chorus of praise, though without robbing music of its
indefinite, inexhaustible character.

♪ ♫ ♪

A third prerogative of the music of eternity will be its ability
to effect in supreme, unsurpassable measure that alliance of
order and love which we so admire in any true masterpiece
here below, especially perhaps in the work of Bach. No more
will there be a conflict, either aesthetically or existentially, between Apollonian and Dionysian elements.[8] Serene transpar-
ency and the balance of repose will be at one with the vital,
vehement energy that rushes forth from the depths of divin-
ized being, finding spontaneous expression in the intoxication
and ecstasy of music. The symphony of the saints will be

---

[7] In support of this assertion, we may remark with Kressmann that
the Bible sometimes uses words for "sing" and "speak" quite indiffer-
ently, as, for example, in Apocalypse 5:9, "they sang a new song and
said . . ." Only after completing the present work did I read the Swiss
philosopher Max Picard's lovely book *The World of Silence* [English translation by Stanley Godman (London: Harvill, [n.d.]) with a preface by
Gabriel Marcel]. The reader will there, notably in the chapter "Silence
as the Origin of Speech," find views that seem to accord with my own.

[8] A distinction drawn from Nietzsche's *Birth of Tragedy*.

marked by neither tragedy nor pathos, yet all that is truly great in tragedy and pathos will resonate within it, bathed in perfect peace, like an immense surge that rises from the bottom of the sea yet spreads upon the surface in gentle ripples. This, I think, is what the music of eternity will be like: inexhaustibly rich in the purity and simplicity of its melodic lines; at once dynamic and calm; both perfectly spontaneous and perfectly ordered.

♪ ♫ ♪

Let us point to one further prerogative. The coexistence of unity and multiplicity that characterizes all true beauty here below will in the music of heaven be pressed to its maximum. Speaking figuratively, the Apocalypse suggests symphonies of unknown dimensions, like the moving sea. We find a wonderful interpretation of this "voice of many waters" in the work of Saint Irenaeus, for whom the waters signify the innumerable paths by which men and women are saved through different economies of grace, all determined by an eternal design of divine mercy.[9] For among the myriad elect, each will have his own voice by which to confess, no less than by his unique "new name" of grace and glory, the novel dispensations of Providence in his regard. Since the body will have become an instrument of expression and communion among the elect, each, in using his own voice, will hear the voices of the rest. As each blends harmoniously with the universal concert, he will read the souls of his fellow men and women in the broad daylight of God. The voice will be the medium by which the elect contemplate the infinite mercy of God to all: the praise of each will be reinforced by that of all the saints. This song of infinite majesty, informed by the glory of him who is its object, is thus not only the song of a limitless universe of spiritual worlds; it is no less a song of profound intimacy, of the most tender exchanges of fraternal love.

[9] *Adv. Haer.* IV.14.

Christ, of course, is the leaven of this solidarity in which the collective and the individual are not opposed but rather strengthen one another. He constitutes the symphony's fullness and triumphant unity in the consonance of a specific chord. His primacy will be truly resplendent once he has completed his work and brought back to the Father the world redeemed by his blood. According to one of the Church Fathers, Christ had from the beginning, as the divine Logos and the Art of God Almighty, attuned man by the Holy Spirit as an instrument fit to sing his Creator's glory: "'You are for me a harp, a flute and a temple,' said he then to man: 'a harp by your harmony, a flute by your breath, and a temple by your reason. The first resonates with, the second breathes, the third shelters the Lord.'"[10]

Man's sin has brought about a terrible dissonance in his own being and in the creation over which he was born to be king. Yet God did not abandon his handiwork. In his love, he wished to "re-create even more wonderfully what he had wonderfully created." That is how Clement of Alexandria shows us the divine and true Orpheus, much more powerful than the pagan deity, using his voice to tame the savage beasts we had become. For while Christ came as the teacher of Israel, he has not abandoned the other peoples of the world. He wants to re-attune us all to his truth, to his love. By pouring out on us the Spirit of sevenfold gift, he has made of our souls a lyre ready to respond to the least stirring from on high. Christ is the New Song arising from the silent abyss of the Father in the eternal *hodie* ["today"] of his generation, and he makes the new song of the redeemed resound on earth: *Gloria in excelsis Deo, et pax hominibus* ["Glory to God in the highest and peace to men"]. At the end of time we shall contemplate him in his glory as the firstfruits of all creation and the firstborn from among the dead, containing in himself all visible

---

[10] Clement of Alexandria, *Protreptikos*, I.5.

and invisible aeons. He will appear as the great Cantor under whose direction and inspiration man recovers his original vocation of praise so as to exercise its full potential. His voice will be our voice, and our voices will be his. How could it be otherwise, since in the unity of one body, now grown to full stature, he is the head while we, in the unity of the Spirit, are one body with him? This is the end of our incorporation into Christ. This is the fruit of the Word's consummated marriage to the Church. Incidentally, is it not significant that the Seer of Patmos uses the expression "voice of many waters" first, at the beginning of the Apocalypse, of Christ in majesty (1:15), then of the vast gathering of the elect (19:6)?

Oh, how it will resound then, that voice of Christ which for love of us once expired![11] How it will be reinforced by our own voices to render all praise to the Father, the final end of the great return! While the unity of earthly music is realized by and through time, the music of heaven will flow from and move within the eternity of the divine Logos, glorious in its unity. Though a symphony of myriad voices, it will have only one voice. Perhaps it will be like a single note, a constant fundamental, within which every conceivable tone, timbre, rhythm, melody and harmony will resonate and finally be resolved?[12]

What, then, will become of our music from here below? Earthly music may well be the echo of a paradise lost and the foretaste of an incomparably lovelier paradise to which we

---

[11] Mark 15:37 (Vulgate): *Iesus autem emissa voce magna exspiravit* ["And Jesus, crying with a loud voice, breathed his last"].

[12] The Bibliothèque Nationale has a precious copy of the *Vie du bienheureux Père Jean de la Croix* by his contemporary and disciple José de Jesús-María (Paris, 1642). In it we find a most curious chapter heading: "How his mind was raised in the manner of an angelic emissary to the celestial music of creation's concord with its Creator." It is a remarkable testimony to a mystical experience which anticipates the eternal music sprung from silence and expressing the harmony of all creatures, visible and invisible, with God: a fruit of Wisdom and of the highest contemplation.

aspire. It may captivate us and free us from ourselves in the intoxication of a Beyond of light and love where the secret of our destiny is concealed. The fact remains, however, that it is a song of exile, the bearer of immense nostalgia. And still, may we not believe that in its pure essence it will not altogether disappear? As a call in the night of infinite Beauty, as the bearer of the highest spiritual values, as a vehicle of grace at the heart of the Church in the service of her cult, music *will* remain, albeit, like everything else, transfigured and fully redeemed by the blood of the Lamb. It is certain that nothing here below can give us an idea of the symphony of glorified souls in which each and every one, impelled by the Word and infused with the Spirit, will be at once inspired composer and amazed listener. Once filled with divine life, once transformed into praise of God, the depth of the soul will give birth to creative life. Man will no longer be a sealed being. Beyond his own frontiers, now fully himself in the sea of God, he will at last be drunk with the free and adequate expression of the spiritual riches that flow within him. They will at last reveal him to himself as one with God and with the whole universe in God.

If at this point we were to speak of rhythm, it could only be that of the *Trisagion* of the angelic powers, which in turn accords with the trinitarian rhythm by which the divine essence knows, loves, and praises itself in engendering, in being engendered, and in breathing forth the Spirit of love, all in the simplicity of energy and in a repose marked by infinite vitality. If we were to speak of melody, it would have to be in the perspective of a single love in flux and reflux. Springing forth from the depths of God to penetrate the depths of the soul and then again returning to its source, it flows in melodic lines of infinite variety, scope, and nuance. Upon the chorus of the redeemed, whose members are beyond counting, it pours out the utter rapture of love that sees the Beloved and is in possession of him. Were we to speak of harmonies, it would be of such that bring the praise of the highest angelic hierarchies into accord with the praise of transfigured creation's lowliest elements. In a concourse of voices at once distinct and wonderfully blended, all these harmonies would echo, and thus make explicit, the great chord of trinitarian praise which for fundamental has the Father, for dominant has the Word-Son, and for mediant, the note by which the other two unite and interpenetrate: the Holy Spirit.

♩ ♫ ♩

From the same perspective (that of the union of opposites), we can point to a final prerogative of the music of eternity. I mean the fact that it is immutable like the God it sings of yet at the same time ever new. The notion of a "new song" seems to correspond to the desire of souls in love, and it is not too far-fetched to believe that it aptly describes the concert of the elect in eternity. Gregory of Nyssa put forward the profound, dizzying view that beatitude is a dynamic, not a static reality. It is characterized at one and the same time by an unchanging, enduring rootedness in God and by a course of progress. For if God himself is unchanging, it is through an excess of movement and life. Within this movement, this life, the blessed will be drawn to discover splendors that never cease to be renewed. The more deeply they penetrate the abyss of Divinity, the more their wonder will grow, for the Divinity, being infinite, remains always equidistant from those whom it never ceases to attract through self-giving.[13] This, then, is what I like

[13] Cf. Jean Daniélou's introduction to the *Life of Moses* in the series *Sources Chrétiennes* (Paris: Cerf, 1955). The doctrine of the eternal discovery of God has been contested, but it is in no way contradicted by Holy Scripture. Furthermore, it is based on solid patristic tradition. Closer to ourselves, we find John of the Cross writing as follows in the fourteenth stanza of his *Spiritual Canticle*: "It is no wonder that God is strange to men who have not seen him, since he is also strange to the holy angels and to the blessed. For the angels and the blessed are incapable of seeing him fully, nor will they ever be capable of doing so. Until the day of the last judgment they will see so many new things in him

to think the music of eternity will be like: inexhaustible, always new, always imbued with the freshness of discovery, and therefore endowed with infinite fecundity and potential.

♪ ♫ ♪

Having reached the end of this enquiry, I cannot help feeling a certain embarrassment before my reader. If a tiny gnat could borrow the voice of an eagle, I would say what Saint Augustine said at the end of his treatise *De Musica*: *Quae potui, sicut potui de tantis, tantillus tecum contuli*: "I have pondered these things with you to the best of my ability, though they are very great and I am very little." Having led us right up to the immensity of eternal life, the mystery of music makes me more aware than ever of my limitations and helplessness. But my misery and nothingness are of little consequence. "Your life," said Saint Ephrem, "is only a drop of water. Direct its course toward God and it will become for you a sea." What may we not hope for from the Life who, for our sake, consented to die on the cross? What may we not hope for from the Love who never ceases to refashion us "with strength and gentleness" in his image so that we, like him, can become love?

---

concerning his deep judgments and his works of mercy and justice that they will forever be receiving new surprises and marveling the more. Hence not only men but also the angels can call him 'strange islands.' Only to himself is he neither strange nor new" (*The Collected Works of St. John of the Cross*, trans. Kieran Kavanaugh and Otilio Rodríguez [London: Nelson, 1966], 465). Among our contemporaries, P. Louvel has written that "Heaven itself resembles a search, or rather it is a developing discovery. Lost in the sea of God, the elect no longer seek, for they have found. Yet they are forever discovering the unsearchable abyss of Divinity, tirelessly going further unto the ages of ages. God is for them the 'Beauty ever old and ever new'" (*La Religion, recherche de Dieu* [Paris: (n. pub.), 1943], 130).

When we transcend ourselves in the sea of God's presence we shall each play our part in the immense spiritual universe of souls. Through it, God will be fully revealed and united to us as to gods: Θεὸς θεοῖς ἑνούμενος τε καὶ γνωριζόμενος.[14] God will praise himself. Here below, meanwhile, it happens rarely and too briefly, in moments that are firstfruits of pure eternity, that the Lord's presence fills us with the indescribable joy of praising him simply because he is. At such times, before a distant horizon that hopelessly escapes us, we receive a fore-taste of what the great waters of eternal music sing:

Gratias agimus tibi, Domine, propter magnam gloriam tuam.
We give you thanks, O Lord, for your great glory!

---

[14] Gregory Nazianzen, *Oratio* XLV.3.